Meek Isn't Weak

The Strength of the Controlled Warrior

BY

Shane W. Cunningham

IRON SHIELD
PRESS

San Antonio, Texas

Library of Congress Control Number: 2025919768

Softcover ISBN: 979-8-9930664-4-8

IRON SHIELD
PRESS

Published by Iron Shield Press
An imprint of 7 Benih Ministry
San Antonio, Texas
www.ironshieldpress.com
www.7benihministry.org

Scripture quotations are taken from the
New American Standard Bible® (NASB),
Copyright © 1960, 1971, 1977, 1995, 2020
by The Lockman Foundation.
Used by permission. All rights reserved.
(www.lockman.org)

Printed in the United States of America

Table of Contents

Chapter 1
Dismissing the Doormat

"A man who doesn't know his own strength can never be meek; he can only be harmless."

LET'S BE HONEST for a minute. When you hear the word "meek," what's the first image that pops into your head?

Go ahead, really think about it.

For most of us, it's not a flattering picture. It's probably a guy with slumped shoulders and downcast eyes. The guy who apologizes when someone else bumps into him. He's the one who gets talked over in meetings, the one whose opinion is always the last to be heard, if it's heard at all. He's passive. He's a pushover.

He's a human doormat.

That's the image, isn't it? And if we're being really honest, there's a part of us that doesn't respect that image. We don't want to be it. As men, we are wired to build, to lead, to protect. We're wired for strength. So when we read that verse, "Blessed are the meek," a wire gets crossed somewhere deep in our souls. It feels like a command to be less than what God made us to be. It feels like a call to weakness.

A Warrior's Dilemma

For years, I believed that lie. In the Marine Corps, the idea of meekness was absurd. It was a fatal flaw. A meek Marine is a dead Marine, and he might take his brothers with him. Everything in our training was designed to forge an aggressive and confident spirit in us. We were taught to be loud, to be decisive, to project strength in our posture, our voice, and our actions. The world, it seemed, belonged to the bold, not the meek.

This created a deep internal conflict when I got out. I wanted to be a good Christian man, but the model of Christian manhood I often saw seemed to be the exact opposite of everything I had been trained to be. It seemed...soft. It seemed like the world had all the warriors, and the church had all the nice guys who wouldn't hurt a fly. How could I reconcile the lion I was trained to be with the lamb I was told I should become?

This is the great lie that has been sold to the Church, and specifically to Christian men. It's one of Satan's most clever deceptions. The strategy is brilliant in its simplicity: take a word that describes a core attribute of a spiritual warrior, twist its meaning into something pathetic, and then watch as an entire generation of men run in the opposite direction, abandoning one of their most powerful assets without even knowing it.

If the enemy can convince you that meekness means weakness, he's effectively neutralized your strength. He has convinced you that to be a good Christian, you have to be a soft man, a man who is passive and ultimately, ineffective. But that's not the mission. That's not the man God calls you to be.

Unlocking the True Definition

The Bible's definition of meekness has absolutely nothing to do with being a doormat. It has nothing to do with timidity or fear. In fact, it's the exact opposite. The key to understanding this is found in a letter from the Apostle Paul, a man who was no stranger to conflict, to his young protégé, Timothy:

For God has not given us a spirit of timidity, but of power and love and discipline (2 Timothy 1:7).

3

Read that again. That's the toolkit God gives every one of his followers. It's not something you have to earn; it's part of your inheritance. Power. Love. Discipline. Notice what's missing? Timidity. Fear. Weakness. The very things the world tries to pin on the word "meek."

This verse isn't just a nice, encouraging platitude. It is the three-legged stool upon which true, biblical meekness rests. Let's break down these God-given tools.

1. A Spirit of Power (Dynamis)

This is the Greek word from which we get "dynamite." This is not a gentle, polite suggestion of strength. This is explosive, world-altering capability. It's the power that flung stars into space. It's the power that rolled the stone away from the tomb. This is the raw material of our strength. It is inherent in our new nature as sons of God.

Too many Christian men live as if they have a thimbleful of power when God has given them an ocean. They pray for God to act, forgetting that the same Spirit who raised Christ from the dead now lives in them. This isn't about arrogance; it's about acknowledging reality. You have been given immense spiritual power. The question is never "Do you have power?" The question is "Do you believe you have it, and how are you directing it?" A man who doesn't know his own strength can never be meek; he can only be harmless.

2. A Spirit of Love (Agape)

If power is the engine, love is the steering wheel. This isn't the sentimental, fluffy feeling from a romantic comedy. This is a rugged, resilient kind of love. It's a fierce commitment to the well-being of others, even at great personal cost. It's the love that makes a man stand between his family and a threat. It's the love that makes a leader put the needs of his team before his own.

This love gives our power a purpose beyond ourselves. A man with power but no love is just a bully. He uses his strength to serve his own ego, to intimidate, and to control. His strength becomes a weapon of destruction. On the other hand, a man with love but no power is just a well-intentioned victim. He has the right motives but lacks the capacity to effect any real change or offer any real protection. The Christian warrior is called to have both: a powerful engine and a steady, selfless hand on the wheel.

3. A Spirit of Discipline (Sophronismos)

This might be the most important word of all for our discussion. It means a sound mind, self-control, sober judgment. It's the ability to see a situation clearly and act wisely. Think of a wild stallion, magnificent in its power, all muscle and energy. It's an incredible creature, but its power is useless, even dangerous. Now think of a trained warhorse, just as powerful, but its strength has been submitted to the will of its rider. It is disciplined. It is controlled. It is effective. That is *sophronismos*.

It's the strong man who has every right to unleash a storm of angry words but has the self-control to remain calm or to offer a gentle answer instead. It's the leader who has the authority to crush a subordinate who made a mistake but has the discipline to use the moment for teaching instead. This is the master switch for meekness. It's the restraint of power. It's the taming of the lion.

The Tamed Lion

Do you see it now? Power, guided by love, and executed with discipline. That is the *biblical* definition of meekness.

It is not the absence of power. It is the disciplined application of immense power for the good of others. The world's meek man is a harmless rabbit, scurrying away from conflict. The Bible's meek man is a tamed lion. He still has all the teeth, all the claws, and all the roar of a king. But he has willingly, voluntarily, placed all of that terrifying power under the authority of his Master. His calmness is not a sign of weakness; it is a sign of incredible control. He doesn't need to roar to prove he's the king, because he knows who he is. His quiet confidence is more intimidating than any empty threat.

So let's dismiss the doormat once and for all. Let's throw that lie on the fire and watch it burn. In this book, we are reclaiming the word meek. We are taking it back from the enemy who twisted it. Because it doesn't belong to the weak, the timid, or the passive.

It belongs to the warrior.

Shane W. Cunningham

Chapter 2
The Enemy Within: Pride

"The insecure man is just as self-obsessed as the arrogant man, but his obsession is focused on his flaws and his image."

BEFORE A BUILDING can be strong, its foundation must be flawless. Before a soldier can be effective, his weapon must be clean. And before a man can be meek, he must identify and declare war on the enemy that occupies his own heart: pride.

If meekness is strength under control, pride is the hairline fracture in the steel. It's the invisible flaw that makes a support beam look solid, right up until the moment it shatters under pressure. From the outside, the proud man can look strong. He might be loud. He might be successful. He might command a certain kind of worldly respect. But on the inside, where it counts, his strength is a facade. It's brittle. It's hollow. And it is destined to fail.

We read in the book of Proverbs, *Pride goes before destruction, and a haughty spirit before stumbling* (Proverbs 16:18). This isn't just a nice moral saying, it's a law of spiritual physics. It's a guaranteed outcome. Pride is the poison that we willingly drink, thinking it makes us stronger, when in reality it is slowly, surely, killing us from the inside out.

But here's the problem. Most of us have a cartoonish understanding of what pride actually is. We think of the preening peacock, the guy who can't stop talking about himself, the arrogant boss who never admits he's wrong. And that is certainly one face of pride. But it's not the only one. Pride is a master of disguise, and to defeat it, we have to be able to recognize it in all its forms.

The Two Faces of Pride

For years, I thought I had a pretty good handle on pride because I wasn't an arrogant guy. I didn't brag, I didn't seek the spotlight. But I was still shot through with pride; it just wore a different uniform. I came to realize that pride isn't just thinking too highly of yourself. In its most basic form, pride is simply thinking of yourself *too much*. It is the spiritual disease of self-obsession. And it shows up in two primary ways.

1. The Loud Pride of Arrogance

This is the face we all know. This is the pride that needs to be the smartest person in the room. It's the voice in our head that whispers, "You deserve the credit for that," or "Don't let them see you don't know the answer." The arrogant man's strength is built on the sandy foundation of comparison. He only feels strong when he feels superior to someone else. Therefore, he is constantly jockeying for position, tearing others down (even subtly) to build himself up. He can't celebrate the success of a friend without a twinge of jealousy. He can't accept criticism, because his sense of self is so fragile that any critique feels like a mortal threat. He is, in a word, brittle. His ego is a thin glass shell. He spends so much energy protecting it that he has no energy left for true service.

2. The Quiet Pride of Insecurity

This is pride's secret weapon. It's the more subtle, more insidious, and for many Christian men, the more dangerous of the two. This is the pride that masquerades as humility.

Years ago, I was in a leadership meeting at work. A major new initiative was being discussed, a project that would require a significant commitment of time and skill. I knew I had the skills to lead it. I had experience in that exact area, but as they asked for a volunteer to step up and take point, I sat in silence. I stared at the table, my hands clasped together.

My thoughts were a swirling storm of self-consciousness. "What if I fail?" "The other guys here are probably more qualified." "If I volunteer, they'll think I'm arrogant, trying to be a big shot." "It's probably better to let someone else do it."

On the surface, it looked like humility. I wasn't seeking the spotlight. I was being quiet and letting others lead. But it was a lie. My silence wasn't rooted in humility; it was rooted in fear. Fear of failure. Fear of judgment. Fear of what others would think of *me*. My entire thought process was about me, me, me. That's the calling card of pride.

The insecure man is just as self-obsessed as the arrogant man, but his obsession is focused on his flaws and his image. His thoughts are a constant loop of self-criticism. "Why did I say that stupid thing?" "Everyone probably thinks I'm an idiot." This quiet pride paralyzes us. It keeps us on the sidelines because we're afraid of what *others will think of us*. A man trapped in quiet pride can't truly serve God or others because he's too busy nursing his own ego and worrying about his own reputation.

Whether it's the loud pride of arrogance or the quiet pride of insecurity, the root is the same: self-obsession. It's a life lived in front of a mirror instead of a window. And a man who is constantly looking at himself cannot possibly follow a Savior who commanded him to look away from himself and follow Him.

The Anatomy of a Fall: A King's Case Study

To see how pride wages war, we need look no further than Israel's first king, Saul. If you were casting a king for a movie, you'd pick Saul. He was tall, handsome, and looked the part. But his heart was eaten through with the termites of pride, and his story is a key example of how it leads to destruction.

Tactic 1: Pride Blinds You. After a key victory, the prophet Samuel gives Saul a direct order from God: wait seven days, and Samuel will come to offer the sacrifice. But the troops get restless. Saul gets nervous. He can't see the bigger spiritual picture; he can only see his immediate political problem. His pride tells him, "You're the king. You have to do something. Your image is on the line." Blinded by fear and self-importance, he disobeys God and offers the sacrifice himself. When Samuel confronts him, Saul is clueless. He can't see his sin. He makes excuses, blames the people, and justifies his disobedience. Pride had put spiritual blinders on him. He was running toward a cliff he was incapable of seeing.

Tactic 2: Pride Isolates You. True strength is forged in brotherhood. David, Saul's successor, surrounded himself with mighty men, with counselors, with prophets who could speak truth to him. Saul, on the other hand, let pride isolate him. He grew jealous of David's success and saw him not as an asset but as a threat. He drove away his own son, Jonathan, because of his friendship with David. He rejected the counsel of the prophet Samuel. The proud man is the loneliest man in the world. He isolates himself because he believes he doesn't need anyone, or he's afraid to let anyone see his weakness. In the end, Saul is left alone on the battlefield, a king with no counsel and no true friends, an easy target for the enemy.

Tactic 3: Pride Makes You Unteachable. This is pride's deadliest tactic. A man who cannot be taught cannot grow. When confronted by Samuel, Saul's first instinct is not repentance, but justification. "But I did obey the voice of the Lord," he argues, even when the evidence (bleating sheep he was supposed to have destroyed) is literally sounding in his ears. He values being right more than he values being obedient. This makes him rigid. His heart hardens. He becomes a man who cannot be corrected, and therefore, cannot be redeemed from his path. This is the tragic end of all pride: it seals you off from the very grace that could save you.

The Antidote: A Field Manual for Humility

Recognizing the enemy is half the battle. The other half is fighting it. You cannot "manage" your pride. You cannot negotiate a truce with it. You must declare total, unconditional, daily war upon it. This isn't about self-hatred; it's about self-forgetfulness. It's about turning the camera away from yourself and pointing it toward God and others.

Here's a practical guide for the fight.

Practice the Art of Asking. The proud man is afraid to ask for help because it's an admission of weakness. The meek warrior knows that asking for help is a sign of strength; it shows you value the mission more than your ego. This week, find one thing you can ask for help with. Ask for directions. Ask a coworker for their input on a project. Ask your wife for her advice on a decision. Every time you ask, you fire a shot at your pride.

Become a Professional Question-Asker. In your next conversation, make it your mission to learn as much as you can about the other person. Ask good questions and then – this is the hard part – shut up and listen. Resist the urge to turn the story back to yourself. The proud man is always waiting for his turn to talk. The meek man is genuinely interested in the story of others.

Seek Out the Truth. Find one or two trusted, godly men in your life. Sit down with them and ask this terrifying question: "Where are my blind spots? What do you see in me that I don't see in myself?" This is the nuclear option against pride. It will hurt. Your ego will scream. But the feedback you receive will be like a surgeon's scalpel, cutting away the cancer of pride so that you can actually heal and grow.

Embrace the Lowly Place. Voluntarily choose to do a task that is "beneath" you. Park in the furthest spot in the parking lot. At a family gathering, be the first one to start clearing the plates. At church, volunteer to clean the toilets or take out the trash. These small, unseen acts of service are like spiritual push-ups. They build the muscle of humility by reminding your ego that your identity is not found in your position, but in your service to the King.

This is the fight of our lives. It's not a one-time decision; it's a thousand small choices every day. Every time you starve your pride and feed your humility, you are strengthening the core of the meek warrior within. You are trading your brittle, hollow facade for the resilient, solid strength of Jesus Christ. And you are preparing yourself for the battles that truly matter.

Chapter 3
The Spoils of War:
Inheriting the Earth

---

*"The world's way is a raw deal.
It promises you ownership but hands
you a life sentence of restless anxiety."*

THERE'S A VERSE in the Bible that sounds like a typo. It's one of those lines that, if we're honest, we usually read right past because it doesn't seem to line up with reality as we know it. Jesus is on a mountainside, giving the most important address in human history, and He drops this bombshell:

"Blessed are the meek, for they shall inherit the earth." (Matthew 5:5)

Let that sink in for a second. The meek. The ones who, as we've established, the world sees as weak and passive. They're the ones who get the grand prize. The whole planet. It just doesn't make sense, does it?

Look around. Who seems to be inheriting the earth right now? It's the aggressive CEOs, the ruthless politicians, the loud-mouthed celebrities, the founders who are willing to crush their competition. The world teaches us that the earth isn't inherited; it's taken. It's conquered. It's seized by force, by ambition, by being smarter, faster, and more relentless than the next guy. The world belongs to the strong, and the world's definition of strong is the exact opposite of meek.

So what are we supposed to do with this verse? Is it just a nice, spiritual sentiment that isn't meant for the real world? Is it a promise for some far-off future when we're all in Heaven? No. It's a promise for right here, right now. But to understand it, we have to realize that Jesus isn't talking about real estate. He's talking about a completely different kind of ownership, a reward so much greater than a title deed or a stock portfolio that they don't even belong in the same conversation.

The Hunger of the Conqueror

The man who sets out to conquer the earth is the hungriest man alive. His entire life is driven by an insatiable need for *more*. More money, more power, more recognition, more stuff. He believes that the next acquisition, the next promotion, the next victory will finally be the thing that satisfies him. But it never is.

His quest is a spiritual hamster wheel. He runs and runs, accumulating more and more, but he never actually arrives anywhere. He's a slave to his own ambition. His possessions end up possessing him. His schedule is a prison. His mind is a constant buzz of anxiety, jealousy, and the gnawing fear that someone else is getting ahead of him. He may look like a king, but he's living like a slave.

This is the great irony. The man who fights to take the earth never actually gets to enjoy it. He's too busy defending his little patch of it, too busy planning his next conquest, too busy worrying about losing what he has. He can't find peace in the present moment because he's forever chasing a future that promises a satisfaction it can never deliver. The world's way is a raw deal. It promises you ownership but hands you a life sentence of restless anxiety.

The Freedom of the Heir

The meek man is on a completely different path. Because his identity is not wrapped up in what he owns or what he controls, he is free. This is the heart of what Jesus is saying. The meek man inherits the earth because he's the only one who is actually free to enjoy it. Let's break down what this inheritance really looks like:

1. You Inherit a Kingdom of Contentment

This is the first, and perhaps most important, piece of your inheritance. The meek man, the warrior who has surrendered his ego to God, is no longer on the hamster wheel. He can get a promotion or lose a job, and his world doesn't fall apart. He can get praise or criticism, and his identity remains stable. Why? Because he's not fighting for his own kingdom anymore. He's a citizen of a greater one.

This brings a profound sense of peace. The proud man is constantly agitated, always grasping. The meek man has a quiet heart. He can take a deep breath and genuinely enjoy the simple gifts of his life - a conversation with his wife, a sunset, a good cup of coffee - because he isn't constantly agitated by the need for more. He possesses his possessions; they don't possess him. This contentment is a treasure that all the money in the world cannot buy. The proud man spends his whole life fighting for a throne, while the meek man inherits a kingdom of peace he can carry inside him everywhere he goes.

2. You Inherit an Empire of Influence

The proud man tries to seize influence through force - his title, his volume, his intimidation. But this is a fragile kind of leadership. His people follow him out of fear, not loyalty. The moment he shows weakness, they're gone.

The meek man builds an empire on a different foundation: trust. His strength isn't loud. It's steady. He's the guy who listens more than he talks. He's the one who gives away the credit. He's the one who admits when he's wrong. He doesn't need to prove he's the alpha, because his security comes from God. And people are desperately drawn to that kind of quiet, stable strength.

His influence grows naturally, without him even trying. His children come to him for advice because they know he'll listen. His coworkers trust his judgment because he has no hidden agenda. People want to be around him because he isn't a threat to them; he's a source of security. Over a lifetime, this quiet, relational influence is infinitely more powerful and lasting than any influence seized by force or position.

3. You Inherit a Territory of Purpose

The man who is fighting for his own patch of earth is consumed by small things: his status, his comfort, his reputation. The meek man, by giving up that small fight, is freed to join a much bigger one.

He inherits a sense of purpose that transcends his own life. His daily work, whether it's on a construction site or in a corner office, becomes part of a divine mission. His family isn't just a responsibility; it's his primary platoon, his legacy. He stops asking, "What can I get?" and starts asking, "What can I give? How can God use my strength to serve and protect others?"

This is the ultimate inheritance. You trade the small, stressful job of building your own little kingdom for the grand, adventurous role of being an ambassador for the King of kings. Your life is no longer about you. It's about something eternal. And there is no greater reward on this earth.

So yes, the meek shall inherit the earth. They trade the anxiety of conquest for the peace of contentment. They trade the fragility of forced authority for the lasting power of trusted influence. They trade the smallness of a self-centered life for the grand adventure of an eternal purpose.

The world sees the meek man as one who is losing. In reality, he's the only one who has already won.

Chapter 4:
The Source of True Power

"It's the ultimate paradox of the
Christian faith: power is not achieved,
it is received. And it is only received
in a state of surrender."

IN EVERY STORY we tell, in every movie we watch, the hero's journey follows a predictable arc. He's tested, he digs deep, he summons a strength he didn't know he had, and he wins the day through sheer force of will. We're taught from a young age that power is something you find inside yourself. It's about gritting your teeth, pushing harder, and relying on your own determination to overcome the odds. The world's message is clear: power comes from within.

And so, we try. We try to be more patient husbands, more disciplined fathers, more honorable men. We read the books, we set the goals, we grit our teeth and resolve to do better this time. And for a little while, it might even work. But then, inevitably, we fail. The anger flares up. The old habits creep back in. The selfish impulse wins the day. We find ourselves, once again, falling short of the men we desperately want to be. And we are left with the frustrating conclusion that the power we have inside ourselves is simply not enough.

This is the point of desperation where the warrior's journey truly begins. It's the moment we finally realize that the world's entire strategy for finding power is a lie. True spiritual strength, the kind of power that produces real, lasting meekness, is not found by digging deeper into ourselves. It is found by giving up on ourselves entirely.

It's the ultimate paradox of the Christian faith: power is not achieved, it is received. And it is only received in a state of surrender.

The Apostle's Secret Weapon

The Apostle Paul was, by any measure, a monster of a man. His intellect was staggering. His physical endurance was legendary. His willpower was seemingly unbreakable. If anyone could have achieved righteousness through sheer self-discipline, it was him. And yet, Paul discovered the secret that we all must learn. He writes about a mysterious "thorn in the flesh," some kind of persistent, painful weakness that plagued him. Three times he begged God to take it away. And God's answer is the key to unlocking all true power.

God said to him, "My grace is sufficient for you, for power is perfected in weakness."

Think about that. Power is *perfected* – brought to its intended, final, most effective state – in weakness. Not in strength. Not in self-reliance. In the admission of absolute, total inadequacy.

Paul's response to this revelation is just as radical. He doesn't despair. He doesn't just tolerate his weakness. He celebrates it. He says,

"Most gladly, therefore, I will rather boast about my weaknesses, so that the power of Christ may dwell in me." (2 Corinthians 12:9).

At first glance, this seems so counterintuitive – boast about weakness? We spend our whole lives trying to *hide* our weaknesses, to project an image of competence and control. Paul is telling us to do the exact opposite. He's saying that our weakness is not a liability; it is our greatest asset. Why? Because it's the very thing that qualifies us to receive God's power.

Imagine a water hose. The water is God's power, his grace. Our pride, our self-reliance, our belief that "I've got this," is like a kink in the hose. It constricts the flow. The moment we say, "God, I *don't* have this. I am weak. I am inadequate. I need you," we are unkinking the hose. The admission of weakness is the act of opening ourselves up to the flow of a power that is not our own.

The Warrior and His Supply Line

A soldier on a mission is only as effective as his supply line. He can be the most highly trained operator in the world, but if he's cut off from food, water, ammunition, and communication with command, he will eventually fail. His strength is not self-contained. It is dependent on a constant connection to a resource much larger than himself.

Our spiritual life works the exact same way. Our supply line is our connection to God. Prayer, scripture, fellowship with other believers - these are the things that keep the supply line open. But enemy number one of the supply line, the saboteur that sneaks in and cuts the line, is pride. And the number one *protector* of the supply line is humility, the conscious admission of weakness.

The man who operates in his own strength is a soldier who has cut his own supply line. He's living off the rations in his pack, and they will eventually run out. This is why we feel so spiritually exhausted. We're trying to fight a war on our own limited resources.

The meek warrior, on the other hand, understands his dependency. His daily prayer is not, "God, help me be strong." It is, "God, *be* my strength." There is a world of difference between those two prayers. The first one assumes the power is still fundamentally ours, we just need a little boost. The second one acknowledges that we have no power to begin with; we are merely a vessel for His.

This dependency doesn't make you weak; it makes you invincible. It means you are no longer limited by your own finite patience, your own finite wisdom, or your own finite strength. You are tapped into an infinite source. When you are humble enough to admit you have no patience left for your kids, you gain access to the inexhaustible patience of God Himself. When you admit you don't have the wisdom to lead your business, you gain access to the wisdom that created the universe.

How to Tap the Source

This all sounds great, but how do we actually live it? It starts by changing the entire orientation of our lives, moment by moment.

The Morning Surrender

Before your feet hit the floor, before you check your phone, before you engage the battles of the day, start with a declaration of dependence. It can be as simple as, "God, I cannot do this day on my own. I have no strength apart from you. Be my strength today. Be my patience. Be my wisdom." Start the day by unkinking the hose.

The In-Battle Whisper

When you're in the middle of a conflict – a stressful meeting, a frustrating conversation with your spouse, a moment of temptation – learn to whisper a prayer of desperation. "God, help." "Jesus, I need you right now." This isn't a sign of failure; it's a tactical masterpiece. It's a real-time activation of your supply line, right when you need it most.

The End-of-Day Inventory

Before you go to sleep, take two minutes to review the day. Where did you operate in your own strength and fail? Confess it. Where did you see God's power show up *after* you admitted weakness? Give thanks for it. This practice trains you to see the connection between your weakness and His power, reinforcing your trust in the system.

This is the source. It's not a secret formula or a seven-step plan. It's a radical, continuous, moment-by-moment exchange: your weakness for His strength. The world tells you to be strong. God tells you to be weak, so that He can show the world what real strength looks like.

Shane W. Cunningham

Chapter 5
Jesus: The Lion in Command

---

*"We must look at both the earth-shaking
roar of the Lion and the world-saving
restraint of the Lamb."*

THERE IS AN image of Jesus that most of us carry around in our heads. It's been curated by centuries of well-meaning but incomplete art, by Sunday School felt boards, and by a cultural desire to domesticate the divine. We see a gentle teacher, serene and soft-spoken, draped in clean white robes. We see a tender shepherd, meek and mild, with a tranquil expression, perhaps holding a lamb. He is approachable, kind, and above all, safe.

And while He is undeniably the Good Shepherd and the embodiment of love, if that gentle image is the only one you have, you are missing the most ferocious and powerful part of the story. You have a sketch, not a portrait. You have a lamb, but you have no lion.

The Jesus of the Bible is not a passive, soft-spoken philosopher who would be comfortable on a modern-day university faculty. He is the most formidable, disruptive, and commanding man who ever walked the earth. He is the Lion of the tribe of Judah, a title that signifies royal authority and terrifying power. His gentleness, the very quality we call meekness, was not a result of a placid personality or an absence of strength. It was the deliberate, disciplined, and moment-by-moment control of *infinite* power.

To truly understand meekness, we must first be willing to be awed, even frightened, by the untamed strength of our King. His meekness is only meaningful when we have some grasp of the cosmic, reality-altering force He was constantly, willfully holding back.

The Apostle Paul, a man who was transformed from a persecutor to a follower by a direct encounter with the resurrected Christ, tried to capture this power in a letter. He wrote:

For by Him all things were created, both in the heavens and on earth, visible and invisible, whether thrones or dominions or rulers or authorities – all things have been created through Him and for Him. He is before all things, and in Him all things hold together. (Colossians 1:16-17).

Let that language sink into your bones. This is our commander. The man who spoke galaxies into existence and who, right now, is the very force holding the atoms of your body together. He is not safe. The idea of a safe lion is a contradiction. But He is good. And if we, as spiritual warriors, want to learn what true strength looks like, we must study His tactics. We must look at both the earth-shaking roar of the Lion and the world-saving restraint of the Lamb.

The Roar of the Lion: Power Unveiled

To appreciate the depth of Jesus's restraint, we must first be staggered by His power. These aren't just miracles or neat party tricks; they are demonstrations of a reality-altering authority. They are moments when the veil is pulled back and we see the true nature of the man from Nazareth.

1. The Cleansing of the Temple: A Strategic Assault

This is one of the most vital and misunderstood events in Jesus's life. It is often downplayed as a moment where He simply "lost His temper," as if the Son of God were prone to petty, emotional outbursts. That is a dangerously shallow reading. This was not an impulsive tantrum; it was a calculated, deliberate, and strategic act of war against a corrupt and oppressive system.

Picture the scene. It's Passover in Jerusalem, the single most important religious festival of the year. The city is flooded with pilgrims. The Temple is the epicenter of the nation's life and worship, the place where heaven and earth were said to meet. But the outer court, the Court of the Gentiles - the one area where non-Jews were permitted to come and pray - had been turned into a noisy, chaotic, and corrupt marketplace.

The air would have been thick with the smell of animals and the stench of greed. The sound was a discord of bleating sheep, lowing oxen, and the sharp, clinking sound of coins. The money changers were there, forcing pilgrims to exchange their Roman currency for Temple currency, at an exorbitant exchange rate. The animal sellers were there, conveniently finding blemishes on the animals the pilgrims brought from home, forcing them to buy an "approved," overpriced animal on site. It was a system of religious extortion, preying on the devotion of the faithful. It was a mockery of God's house.

And into this scene walks Jesus. He doesn't form a committee. He doesn't write a letter to the Sanhedrin. He takes decisive, personal, and physical action. John's gospel tells us He made a whip of cords. Think about the profound intentionality of that simple act. He didn't just grab a stick in a fit of rage. He sat down. He gathered the cords. He took the time to braid them together. This was a premeditated act, fueled by a holy and righteous anger.

Then, He unleashes His assault. He single-handedly, in a display of absolute authority, drives out all the merchants and their animals. He overturns their tables, the symbols of their corrupt enterprise, and sends their ill-gotten coins scattering across the stone floor. He roars,

"Take these things away; stop making My Father's house a place of business." (John 2:16).

Do not miss the sheer audacity and power of this moment. He wasn't just taking on a few vendors. He was taking on the entire corrupt, entrenched financial and religious system of his day. These were powerful men, protected by the Temple guard and sanctioned by the high priest. Yet, no one stops him. The guards, the authorities, the merchants – they are all stunned into submission by the sheer force of His personal authority. In that moment, they weren't dealing with a gentle carpenter from a backwoods town. They were dealing with a King reclaiming His rightful territory. This was not a moment of weakness or emotional failure. This was the roar of the Lion, cleansing His den.

2. The Command of the Creator: Reality Obeys

Throughout His ministry, Jesus demonstrated a power that belonged only to God. He didn't ask creation to cooperate; He commanded it. The most famous example is the storm on the Sea of Galilee. His disciples, several of whom were expert fishermen who knew that sea like the back of their hand, are in a full-blown panic. They are convinced they are about to die. Jesus, awakened from a nap in the stern of the boat, simply stands and speaks to the non-sentient elements of wind and water. He says, *"Peace, be still."*

The text says the wind immediately ceased and there was a great calm. The disciples were no longer afraid of the storm; they were now terrified of the man in their boat. They asked each other, "Who then is this, that even the wind and the sea obey Him?" It was the right question.

But His authority wasn't limited to weather patterns. He demonstrated power over the very substance of reality. He took five loaves of bread and two fish and fed a crowd of over five thousand people, with baskets of leftovers. He walked on top of the water, defying the laws of physics. His authority extended to the biological realm. He healed the sick, gave sight to the blind, and made the lame walk, often with just a word or a touch. His power even extended over death itself, culminating in His command to a man who had been dead for four days: *"Lazarus, come forth."* And the dead man walked out of his tomb. He didn't just have authority in creation; He was the authority *over* creation.

3. The Dismantling of the Proud: Intellectual Dominance

Jesus's power wasn't just supernatural; it was intellectual and verbal. He consistently engaged the most educated, cunning, and powerful religious leaders of His day - the Pharisees, Sadducees, and scribes - and in every single encounter, He verbally and logically dismantled them.

They came to Him constantly with trick questions, designed to trap Him. If He answered one way, He would alienate the people. If He answered the other way, He would be breaking Roman or Jewish law. It was a continuous series of intellectual ambushes. And every time, Jesus not only sidestepped their trap but turned it back on them, using their own logic to expose the darkness and hypocrisy of their hearts.

Consider the famous trap regarding taxes. They asked Him, *"Is it lawful to give a poll-tax to Caesar, or not?"* If He said yes, He would be seen as a traitor to the Jewish people, collaborating with their Roman oppressors. If He said no, He could be immediately arrested for treason against Rome. It was a perfect trap.

Jesus asked for a coin. He held it up and asked, *"Whose likeness and inscription is this?"* They answered, "Caesar's."

His response was a stroke of tactical genius that left them speechless:

"Then render to Caesar the things that are Caesar's; and to God the things that are God's." (Matthew 22:21).

With one sentence, He affirmed civic duty without compromising spiritual loyalty. He avoided their trap, laid a profound theological principle, and left his opponents standing in stunned silence. He did this time and time again. He was not just a wise teacher spouting beatitudes. He was a master of debate, a brilliant strategist, and an intellectual warrior who could not be defeated.

The Restraint of the Lion: Power Controlled

If that was the only side of Jesus we saw, we would have a model for dominance, but not for meekness. It is in His restraint, in the moments when He *could* have unleashed His infinite power but *chose* not to, that we find our most profound and challenging lesson. This is where the warrior finds his true north.

1. The Garden of Gethsemane: The Unsummoned Army

This is the ultimate classroom for the meek warrior. Jesus is in the garden, having just prayed a prayer of such agony that He sweat drops of blood. He is in submission to His Father's will, but the human cost is immense. Then, the torchlights appear. The Temple guards arrive with Judas to arrest Him.

Peter, ever the man of action, does what any warrior would do when his commander is threatened: he draws his sword and prepares to fight. He lunges and, in the chaos, cuts off the ear of the high priest's servant. It's a moment of worldly, well-intentioned, but ultimately misguided strength.

And Jesus immediately shuts it down. He rebukes Peter and miraculously heals the servant's ear - an act of grace to an enemy in the very act of aggression. Then He says something to Peter that should shake us to our core:

"Do you think that I cannot appeal to My Father, and He will at once put at My disposal more than twelve legions of angels?" (Matthew 26:53).

Let's not read past that number. A Roman legion at full strength was about 6,000 soldiers. Twelve legions is over 72,000 angels. We have to understand what that means. In the Old Testament, a single angel was dispatched to deal with the Assyrian army threatening Jerusalem, and in one night, that one angel killed 185,000 enemy soldiers. We cannot even begin to comprehend the scale of the cataclysmic, destructive power Jesus had at His immediate disposal. He could have vaporized the entire cohort of Roman and Temple guards, flattened the city of Jerusalem, and ended the rebellion against His kingship in a single, fiery instant.

And yet, standing there, betrayed by a friend, facing an unjust arrest that He knew would lead to His torture and execution, He chooses not to make the call.

That is meekness. It is not weakness. It is not passivity. It is the deliberate restraint of overwhelming power in absolute submission to a higher mission. Peter's strength could save Jesus from a cross. Jesus's strength, expressed through meekness, could save the entire world. He chose the greater mission.

2. The Silence of the King: Authority in Submission

Throughout His sham trials, Jesus is mostly silent. He stands before Pilate, the Roman governor. Pilate is a man who holds the power of life and death in his hands. He is the face of Roman imperial might. Exasperated by Jesus's quiet dignity, Pilate tries to intimidate Him, saying, "Do You not know that I have authority to release You, and I have authority to crucify You?"

Jesus's reply is one of the most powerful and chilling lines in Scripture. He looks at this powerful governor and says,

"You would have no authority over Me, unless it had been given you from above." (John 19:11).

In that moment, the roles are reversed. The prisoner reminds the judge who is actually in charge. Jesus is not a victim of circumstance, tossed about by the whims of corrupt politicians. He is a King, willingly and purposefully submitting Himself to a broken system to achieve a divine purpose. He could have ended the trial with a single word. He could have called witnesses from heaven to testify. He could have revealed a glimpse of His glory and sent Pilate to his knees in terror. He chose silence. He chose restraint.

3. The Forgiveness from the Cross: The Ultimate Power Move

The ultimate demonstration of meekness, of strength under perfect control, comes at the cross. As He hangs, nailed to the wood, the life draining from Him, He is subjected to the absolute worst of humanity. He is mocked by the religious leaders, ridiculed by the soldiers, and scorned by one of the criminals being crucified beside him.

His power is still absolute. His connection to the Father is still intact. He could have, even then, called down the legions of angels. He could have cursed His enemies. He could have ended His suffering and brought righteous judgment upon them all.

Instead, He looks down at the very people who have tortured Him and are in the process of killing Him, and He prays. He uses some of His last, precious breaths to say,

"Father, forgive them; for they do not know what they are doing." (Luke 23:34).

To absorb that level of injustice, pain, and betrayal – to take the full, concentrated force of human hatred – and to respond not with righteous fury but with grace-filled forgiveness is the greatest act of strength in the history of the universe. It is a strength that shatters every worldly definition of power. It is the power to absorb evil and not return it, to suffer for the sake of love, to win a war not by killing your enemies, but by dying for them.

This is our model. This is our King. Jesus was not weak; He was the strongest man who ever lived. He was not passive; He was the most courageous and decisive man who ever lived. His meekness was His infinite strength, perfectly bridled by His infinite love and His unwavering commitment to His Father's mission. He is the Lion in command. And He calls us, as His spiritual warriors, to learn from Him - to cultivate true, God-given strength, and then to learn to bridle it in humble, courageous service to our King and His world-saving mission.

Chapter 6
David: The King in Waiting

"David's meekness teaches us to do our part with excellence and then trust God with the promotion and the timing."

IF JESUS IS the perfect, divine model of meekness, David is our flawed but faithful human example. He is perhaps the most compelling case study in all of Scripture for what it looks like to be a "monster" - a man of immense capacity for violence, passion, and leadership - who learns to bring that monstrous capability under the control of God.

David's life is a story of contrast. He is a poet and a warrior. A shepherd and a king. A man of soaring faith and devastating failure. And it is in this messy, human reality that we find our most relatable lessons. We see in David a man who could have seized power, justified revenge, and taken what he was promised by force. But in his defining moments, he chose a different path. He chose the warrior's path of meekness, demonstrating that true strength lies not in taking power, but in restraining it until it is given by God.

To understand the miracle of David's restraint, we must first understand the ferocity of the man. He was not a soft boy playing a harp in a field. He was a killer, forged in the wilderness and proven on the battlefield.

The Forging of a Warrior

Long before he was a king, David was a shepherd. In our modern world, we picture a shepherd as a gentle, passive figure. That is not the reality of shepherding in ancient Israel. A shepherd was the sole protector of his flock in a hostile wilderness filled with predators. David wasn't just counting sheep; he was defending them with his life.

He tells King Saul, with no hint of boasting but with a simple statement of fact, what this job entailed:

"Your servant was tending his father's sheep. When a lion or a bear came and took a lamb from the flock, I went out after him and attacked him, and rescued it from his mouth; and when he rose up against me, I seized him by his beard and struck him and killed him." (1 Samuel 17:34-35).

Stop and picture this scene. This is a teenage boy, armed with nothing but a staff and a slingshot, hunting down a lion.

Not just scaring it away, but chasing it, engaging it in hand-to-paw combat, and killing it. He does the same with a bear. This is not normal. This is a display of breathtaking courage and raw physical power. From his youth, David possessed a warrior's spirit and a capacity for violence that set him apart. He knew how to kill.

This raw capability is put on public display in the Valley of Elah. The story of David and Goliath is so famous that we've sanitized it. We see it as a cute story about an underdog. It is a story of a calculated, lethal takedown by a skilled warrior.

While the entire army of Israel, including its king, is cowering in fear of the giant Goliath, David is offended. Not just scared, but deeply, spiritually offended that this "uncircumcised Philistine" is defying the armies of the living God. His anger is righteous. He approaches Saul, not with a plea, but with a resume of his past victories over lions and bears. He is confident in his God, yes, but he is also confident in his skill set.

He rejects the king's heavy, cumbersome armor. This is not an act of naive faith; it is the choice of a specialist. David is a projectile weapons expert. He knows that his strength lies in speed, movement, and precision, not in brute force. He walks onto that battlefield with five smooth stones and a sling. A sling was not a child's toy. In the hands of an expert, it was a deadly weapon, capable of launching a projectile at over 100 miles per hour with pinpoint accuracy.

Goliath mocks him. David responds with one of the greatest battle cries in history, declaring that he comes in the name of the Lord of Hosts. Then, the action. David runs *toward* the giant. He doesn't wait. He doesn't hesitate. He closes the distance, slings the stone, and hits Goliath in the one small, unarmored spot on his forehead. The giant falls. But David isn't done. He runs up, takes Goliath's own massive sword, and cuts off his head.

This is the man we are dealing with. A courageous, skilled, and utterly lethal warrior. He is a national hero. He has been anointed by the prophet Samuel to be the next king. He has the promise of God, the love of the people, and the skill to back it up. He is, by any definition, a monster of capability.

And for the next decade, he does nothing to claim the throne. Instead, he runs for his life.

The Pressure of the Wilderness

David's victory makes him a hero to the people, but it makes him a threat to the insecure and crumbling King Saul. Saul is consumed by a bitter, paranoid jealousy. He is the man who has the crown, but he knows David has the anointing.

And so, the king begins a relentless campaign to murder the young hero.

Saul tries to kill him with a spear, not once, but twice, while David is literally playing the harp to soothe the king's troubled mind. He sends David on impossible military missions, hoping he will be killed by the Philistines. When that fails, he begins a full-scale manhunt, chasing David and his growing band of followers through the desolate wilderness of Judah.

For years, David lives as a fugitive. He hides in caves, scrambles over rocks, and lives on the run. He is the rightful king, living like a hunted animal, pursued by the man who is wrongfully sitting on his throne. During this time, a group of men gathers around him. The Bible describes them as

"Everyone who was in distress, and everyone who was in debt, and everyone who was discontented." (1 Samuel 22:2).

This is a band of outcasts, rebels, and hardened men. And David, the charismatic warrior, forges them into an elite fighting force known as David's Mighty Men.

This is a critical point. David is not a lone fugitive. He is a commander. He has a private army of loyal, lethal warriors at his disposal. He has the means, the motive, and the popular support to launch a civil war and take the throne that is rightfully his. Every worldly instinct would tell him to fight back, to claim his destiny, to put an end to the unjust persecution he is enduring.

And this is where David's true battle begins. It is not a battle against Saul. It is a battle against the desires of his own heart and the voices of his own men. It is the battle for meekness.

The Test in the Cave

The ultimate test comes in the wilderness of En Gedi. David and his men are hiding deep in the back of a massive cave. And who should walk in, alone, but King Saul. The Bible tells us he entered the cave "to relieve himself." He is vulnerable, unsuspecting, and completely at David's mercy.

The cave must have been electric with tension. David's men see this as a clear sign from God. Their whispers are urgent, a temptation to action:

"Behold, this is the day of which the LORD said to you, 'Behold, I am about to give your enemy into your hand, and you shall do to him as it seems good to you.'" (1 Samuel 24:4).

Everything is aligned for David to act. He has the justification - Saul has tried to murder him repeatedly. He has the opportunity - Saul is alone and vulnerable. He has the encouragement of his followers. He has the promise of the throne. All he has to do is give the signal. His men would have killed Saul in an instant, and the kingdom would be his.

And what does David do? He creeps forward in the darkness. He gets close enough to Saul to feel his breath. He has a knife in his hand. And he cuts off a corner of Saul's robe. A symbolic act. A way to prove he was there, that he could have killed him.

But even this small act of disrespect floods him with guilt. The Scripture says,

"It came about afterward that David's conscience bothered him because he had cut off the corner of Saul's robe."

He goes back to his men, his heart pounding, and he gives them a command that must have stunned them into silence.

"Far be it from me because of the LORD that I should do this thing to my lord, the LORD'S anointed, to stretch out my hand against him, since he is the LORD'S anointed." (1 Samuel 24:6).

He doesn't just decide this for himself; he actively prevents his men from attacking Saul. He bridles not only his own power but the power of his entire army. This is meekness in action. It is strength under perfect control, submitted to a higher principle. David's principle was this: Saul may be my enemy, but he is still God's anointed king. It is God's job to remove him, not mine. My job is to wait.

After Saul leaves the cave, David goes out and calls to him. He bows his face to the ground in a sign of respect. He holds up the piece of robe as evidence, not of his power, but of his innocence and loyalty. He makes his case, not with a sword, but with a humble appeal. The act so disarms Saul that the tormented king weeps, acknowledging David's righteousness and his own sin. For a moment, David's meekness has done what all his fighting prowess could never do: it has conquered the king's heart.

The Second Test: Proof of Character

One instance could be a fluke. A moment of clarity. But true character is revealed through consistency. God gives David a second test, almost a replay of the first.

Sometime later, Saul is again hunting David. David and one of his fiercest lieutenants, Abishai, sneak into Saul's camp in the dead of night. They walk past the sleeping guards and find the king himself, fast asleep, with his spear stuck in the ground by his head.

Abishai, a man of action, sees this as a second chance from God to finish the job. His whisper is even more direct than the men in the cave.

"God has delivered your enemy into your hand today; now therefore, please let me strike him with the spear to the

ground with one stroke, and I will not strike him a second time." (1 Samuel 26:8).

He is promising a clean, swift kill. No mess, no fuss. Just one quick action to end the war.

And again, David refuses. His reasoning is exactly the same. *"Do not destroy him, for who can stretch out his hand against the LORD'S anointed and be without guilt?"*

Instead, he tells Abishai to simply take Saul's spear and his water jug. They sneak back out of the camp, and from a safe distance, David again confronts Saul's army, holding up the proof of his mercy. He had the king's life in his hands, twice, and both times he chose restraint. He proved that his meekness was not a one-time decision but the settled condition of his heart.

Lessons from the King-in-Waiting

David's story in the wilderness is a display of mastery for the modern spiritual warrior. It provides a clear set of tactical principles for our own lives:

Meekness Trusts God's Timing

David had the promise, but he was willing to wait for God's timing. He could have taken a shortcut to the throne, but he knew that a throne seized by force would have to be maintained by force. He chose to wait for God to hand it to him. How often do we try to force a promotion, a relationship, or an outcome in our own lives? David's meekness teaches us to do our part with excellence and then trust God with the promotion and the timing.

Meekness Honors God-Given Authority

David's restraint was rooted in his respect for the *office* of the king, even when the *man* in that office was corrupt and trying to kill him. This is an incredibly difficult principle. It's easy to respect a good boss, a wise pastor, or a just leader. But David's example challenges us to show respect to the position of authority, even when we disagree with the person holding it, trusting that God is the one who ultimately raises up and puts down leaders.

Meekness Is an Offensive Weapon

In both encounters, David's act of mercy completely disarmed Saul. It exposed Saul's sin and highlighted David's righteousness in a way that no act of violence ever could. A gentle answer turns away wrath. An act of mercy can break an enemy's spirit. We think of retaliation as strength, but David shows us that a calculated, deliberate act of non-retaliation can be the most powerful strategic move a warrior can make.

David, the giant-slayer, the lion-killer, the commander of armies, found that his greatest strength was not in his sword arm, but in his bridled heart. He was a monster of a man who willingly put a leash on his own power, submitting it to the will and timing of God. And in doing so, he became a king for the ages, and a man after God's own heart.

Shane W. Cunningham

Chapter 7
Saul: When Strength Becomes Brittle

---

*"The moment he felt that control slipping,
the cracks in his character began to show."*

IN EVERY GREAT story, the hero's journey is illuminated by the shadow of another. It's the contrast that gives the picture its depth. To fully appreciate the resilient, flexible strength of a warrior like David, we must place his story alongside that of a man who was his polar opposite. We must perform an autopsy on a different kind of king.

We need to talk about Saul.

Saul's story is one of the great tragedies of the Bible. It's crucial that we don't just see him as a one-dimensional villain. He wasn't born a monster. He was chosen by God. He was a man blessed with every external advantage, a man who had the potential for greatness. But his story serves as a chilling cautionary tale for every spiritual warrior. It is a detailed, slow-motion account of how strength without meekness becomes brittle.

Saul represents the man who looks the part, who has the perfect resume, but who lacks the inner core of humble trust that allows a leader to bend without breaking. His strength was built on the shaky ground of human approval and his own ability to control his circumstances. When that ground shifted, his impressive exterior cracked, revealing the hollow insecurity within. He is the warrior who shines on the parade ground but shatters in the chaos of a real battle. His life is a warning: strength without a submitted heart is not strength at all; it is simply a prelude to a fall.

The Perfect Resume: A King for the People

When we first meet Saul, he seems like the perfect candidate for Israel's first king. In a world that judges by outward appearance, Saul was a masterpiece. The text of 1 Samuel introduces him with a description that sounds like it was written by a casting director looking for a leading man.

First, he had the look. The Bible tells us he was from a wealthy and influential family. More than that, he was physically breathtaking. The scripture says,

"There was not a more handsome person than he among the sons of Israel; from his shoulders and up he was taller than any of the people." (1 Samuel 9:2).

Let's not underestimate the power of this. In a warrior culture, size and stature matter. He commanded respect simply by walking into a room. When the people saw him, they saw a king. He looked powerful, he looked capable, he looked like a man who could lead an army. He was, in modern terms, a "natural leader."

Second, he had a humble start. When the prophet Samuel first hints at his destiny, telling him, "On whom is all the desire of Israel? Is it not on you and on all your father's house?", Saul's response is one of apparent humility. He says,

"Am I not a Benjamite, from the smallest of the tribes of Israel, and my family the least of all the families of the tribe of Benjamin? Why then have you spoken this word to me?" (1 Samuel 9:21).

This sounds like the perfect answer. It sounds like a man who knows his place, who isn't grasping for power. Later, when the lots are cast and he is publicly chosen as king, he can't even be found. He's hiding among the baggage. Again, this appears to be a sign of a man not puffed up with pride.

Third, he was chosen by God. This wasn't a military coup or a political power grab. Saul was anointed by Samuel, the most respected prophet in the land. The Spirit of God came upon him. He had a divine mandate for his rule.

Finally, he had early success that validated his calling. In his first test as king, the Ammonites besiege the city of Jabesh-Gilead, threatening to gouge out the right eye of every man. It's a brutal, terrorizing threat. When Saul hears the news, the Spirit of God comes upon him mightily. He acts with swift, decisive, and furious energy. He rallies the nation, leads a daring surprise attack, and wins a resounding victory, saving the city. In the aftermath, some of his supporters want to execute the men who had initially doubted his kingship. But Saul shows mercy, saying,

"Not a man shall be put to death this day, for today the LORD has accomplished deliverance in Israel." (1 Samuel 11:13).

The resume is perfect. He has the physical presence, the initial humility, the divine anointing, and a proven track record of victory and mercy. By all external measures, he is the ideal king. So where did it all go so terribly wrong? The answer is that his strength was never tested by the one thing that forges true character: waiting.

The Cracks Begin to Show:
Strength Without Submission

A piece of steel is made strong through a process of heating and cooling. It's the pressure and the waiting that gives it its temper. Saul's character was never properly tempered. His strength was impressive, but it had a fatal flaw: it was entirely dependent on his ability to be in control. The moment he felt that control slipping, the cracks in his character began to show.

1. The Impatient Sacrifice: A Failure of Trust

The first major crack appears at Gilgal. Saul and his fledgling army are facing a terrifying Philistine force, a massive army with thousands of chariots. Saul is supposed to wait seven days for Samuel to arrive and offer the pre-battle sacrifices to God. This is a direct command from the prophet.

The pressure is immense. The Philistine army is gathering. And Saul's own men, seeing the overwhelming odds, are beginning to panic and desert. The text says they were "hiding in caves, in thickets, in cliffs, in cellars, and in pits." Saul feels his control of the situation slipping away by the hour. He can see his army dissolving before his eyes.

Samuel is late. The seventh day arrives, and still no prophet. Saul's anxiety boils over. He can't wait any longer. He has to *do something* to restore morale and seize back control.

So he makes a fatal decision. He violates a direct command and takes matters into his own hands, offering the burnt offering himself - a sacred duty reserved for the prophet.

Just as he finishes, Samuel arrives. The prophet's question is simple and devastating: *"What have you done?"*

Saul's excuse is a classic example of a man justifying his disobedience. He blames his circumstances: "I saw that the people were scattering from me, and that you did not come within the appointed days, and that the Philistines were assembling." He blames his fear: "I said, 'Now the Philistines will come down against me... and I have not asked the favor of the LORD.'" And then the final, damning statement:

"So I forced myself and offered the burnt offering." (1 Samuel 13:12).

This was not a failure of courage. It was a failure of trust. A meek warrior, a man like David, would have understood that his true strength lay not in his army or his own actions, but in his obedience to God. David would have waited, trusting that God's timing was more important than his own tactical assessment. Saul, whose strength was rooted in his ability to control the situation, panicked when he lost that control. He chose the appearance of leadership over the substance of obedience. And in that moment, Samuel delivers a heartbreaking verdict: *"You have acted foolishly... your kingdom shall not endure."*

2. The Incomplete Obedience: A Failure of Submission

God, in His grace, gives Saul another chance to prove his heart. He is given a second major command, a chance to show that he has learned his lesson. This time, the command is even more direct and severe. He is to execute God's judgment on the Amalekites, an ancient and wicked enemy of Israel.

The command, delivered through Samuel, is brutally clear:

"Now go and strike Amalek and utterly destroy all that he has, and do not spare him; but put to death both man and woman, child and infant, ox and sheep, camel and donkey." (1 Samuel 15:3).

This is a difficult command, but it is unambiguous. There is no room for interpretation.

Saul obeys, but only partially. He leads the army, wins the battle, and destroys the Amalekite people. But he makes two critical exceptions. He spares Agag, the king of the Amalekites, likely to parade him as a trophy of war. And he and his army keep the best of the sheep, oxen, and other livestock.

When Samuel comes to confront him, Saul greets him with a cheerful and self-deceiving declaration: *"Blessed are you of the LORD! I have carried out the command of the LORD."*

Samuel's response is one of the most haunting lines in the Old Testament: *"What then is this bleating of the sheep in my ears, and the lowing of the oxen which I hear?"*

Saul's house of cards comes tumbling down. His excuses are a textbook case of pride and blame-shifting. First, he blames the people: *"The people spared the best of the sheep and oxen..."* A true leader takes responsibility; a brittle one points fingers. Second, he tries to spiritualize his disobedience: They kept the animals *"to sacrifice to the LORD your God at Gilgal."* He tries to justify his sin by wrapping it in a religious cloak. He thinks a good idea (offering a massive sacrifice) can substitute for a direct command.

This is the moment of final judgment for Saul's kingship. Samuel's rebuke cuts to the very heart of the difference between Saul's brittle strength and the resilient strength of meekness:

"Has the LORD as much delight in burnt offerings and sacrifices as in obeying the voice of the LORD? Behold, to obey is better than sacrifice, and to heed than the fat of rams. For rebellion is as the sin of divination, and insubordination

is as iniquity and idolatry. Because you have rejected the word of the LORD, He has also rejected you from being king." (1 Samuel 15:22-23).

Saul's strength led him to believe he knew better than God. He valued the spoils of war, the approval of his soldiers, and his own "good idea" more than the clear, simple, and difficult command of his God. This is pride in its purest form. It is the belief that our plan is better than God's. And it is the crack that shatters a king.

The Shattering: The Fruits of a Brittle Heart

Once rejected by God, the Spirit of the Lord departs from Saul, and his descent accelerates. The strength he once had, now detached from its divine source, curdles into a toxic mix of jealousy, paranoia, and fear.

It begins with a song. After David kills Goliath, the women of Israel sing a simple, catchy tune: *"Saul has slain his thousands, and David his ten thousands."* For a meek man, a leader secure in his identity, this would be a moment of pride. He would celebrate the success of his champion, knowing that David's victory was a victory for the whole nation.

But for Saul, whose sense of self was built on being number one, this song is an existential threat. The text says,

"Saul was very angry... and he said, 'They have ascribed to David ten thousands, but to me they have ascribed thousands. Now what more can he have but the kingdom?' So Saul eyed David with suspicion from that day on." (1 Samuel 18:8-9).

His insecurity explodes into a consuming jealousy. That jealousy quickly festers into paranoid violence. Twice, while David is playing the harp to soothe him, Saul hurls a spear at him, trying to pin him to the wall. His strength, once used to fight Israel's external enemies, is now turned inward against its greatest hero. He becomes obsessed, dedicating the vast resources of the kingdom to hunting this one young man.

Pride isolates. Saul drives away everyone who could help him. He alienates his own son, Jonathan, who loves David. He turns against his own daughter, Michal, who helps David escape. He orders the massacre of the priests at Nob for simply giving David bread. He is left alone, surrounded by sycophants, consumed by his own fear.

The final, tragic act of his life reveals how far he has fallen. On the eve of his last battle against the Philistines, terrified and abandoned by God, Saul seeks out a medium, a witch at Endor, to summon the spirit of the dead prophet Samuel. The man who began his reign as God's anointed king ends his life seeking counsel from the very demonic sources God had explicitly forbidden. It is the ultimate act of a man who cannot humble himself and will desperately seek power from any source *but* the one true God. He dies the next day on the battlefield, a broken and defeated king.

The Legacy of a Broken King

Saul's life is a mirror held up to the warrior heart. It shows us a man who had strength, but not meekness. He had courage, but not trust. He had authority, but not submission.

David, the monster of capability, willingly put a leash on his power and waited for God's timing. Saul, the impressive but hollow king, could not bear to not be in control and tried to force God's hand. David's strength was resilient, able to withstand years of pressure in the wilderness because it was rooted in God's approval. Saul's strength was brittle, shattering at the first sign of pressure because it was rooted in his own performance and the approval of the people.

The tragedy of Saul is that the "Saul" in all of us is a constant threat. It is the voice that tells us to value appearance over substance. It is the impulse to take control rather than to trust. It is the temptation to believe that our good ideas are an acceptable substitute for God's clear commands.

Saul's story is not in the Bible to make us feel superior. It is there as a solemn and terrifying warning. It shows that a warrior without meekness, no matter how handsome, how talented, or how successful he appears to be, is destined to break. True strength, the kind that endures the battle and outlasts the grave, is the strength that kneels.

Chapter 8
Moses: The General Who Knelt

---

*"I AM WHO I AM... Say to the sons of
Israel, 'I AM has sent me to you.'"
(Exodus 3:14).*

THERE ARE SOME figures in history so monumental that their names alone conjure images of power. Moses is one of them. We see him in our mind's eye, a man of rugged, commanding presence. We see him with his staff raised, the Red Sea parting before him. We see him, face aglow, descending a smoking mountain with stone tablets in his arms. We see him confronting the Pharaoh of Egypt, the most powerful man in the known world, and bringing that empire to its knees. He is a lawgiver, a prophet, a nation-builder, a general.

He is the very definition of a strong leader.

And that is why the single greatest description of his character in the entire Bible is so jarring, so utterly disruptive to our modern ideas of strength. It comes in the middle of a story about a leadership challenge from his own family. After describing their complaint, the Holy Spirit pauses the narrative to give us a divine editorial note, a piece of character analysis that we are clearly meant to stop and wrestle with. It says:

Now the man Moses was very meek, more than any man who was on the face of the earth. (Numbers 12:3).

Read that again. The meekest man on earth. Not one of the meekest. *The* meekest.

How can this be? How can the man who called down plagues, who led a nation through the wilderness, who spoke with God as a man speaks to a friend, be defined by meekness? This isn't just a paradox; it is the key to understanding the entire operating system of a spiritual warrior. Moses' life proves that supernatural power does not flow *in spite of* meekness. It flows *because of* it.

Moses' story is the story of two different lives. The first forty years are the story of a man being built up by the world, trained in self-reliance and worldly power. The next forty years are the story of God patiently dismantling that man in the desolate silence of the desert. It was only after Moses was broken of his own strength that he was ready to be used by God's. He had to fail as a prince before he could succeed as a prophet. He had to learn the weakness of his own hands before he could become a conduit for the power of God's.

The Self-Reliant Prince: A Strength that Kills

To appreciate the meekness of the 80-year-old Moses who stood before a burning bush, we have to understand the self-reliant strength of the 40-year-old prince who stood in the courts of Pharaoh.

Moses' early life is the stuff of legend. Born a Hebrew slave under a death sentence, he is miraculously saved and adopted into the very house of the king who ordered his death. He is raised as the grandson of Pharaoh. The book of Acts tells us,

"Moses was educated in all the wisdom of the Egyptians, and he was powerful in speech and action." (Acts 7:22).

Do not underestimate what this means. He would have received the finest military, political, and academic training the world's greatest superpower could offer. He understood strategy, logistics, and leadership. He was a man of immense privilege and, by all accounts, immense capability. He was powerful. He was a somebody.

And he had a righteous heart. He saw the suffering of his Hebrew brethren, and it stirred something in him. He knew he was one of them, and he felt the call to be their deliverer. The stage is set. We have a righteous man with a righteous cause, who possesses the power and position to do something about it. It seems like the perfect formula for a hero.

And it leads to disaster.

His first attempt at deliverance is not a grand political movement or a strategic military campaign. It's an act of impulsive, personal violence. He sees an Egyptian taskmaster brutally beating a Hebrew slave. The injustice ignites his anger. The text says,

"He looked this way and that, and when he saw there was no one, he struck down the Egyptian and hid him in the sand." (Exodus 2:12).

This is worldly strength in action. It's a man taking matters into his own hands. He has the power to kill, so he uses it. He has a righteous motive, but his method is entirely his own. The phrase "he looked this way and that" is so telling. He is checking for human witnesses, but he has not consulted his divine Commander. This is a solo operation.

He thinks this act will establish him as the champion of his people. He assumes they will see him as their deliverer. The next day, he tries to break up a fight between two Hebrews, and his self-appointed leadership is immediately and brutally rejected. One of them shoves him aside and asks a question that shatters his entire identity: *"Who made you a prince and a judge over us? Are you intending to kill me as you killed the Egyptian?"*

The news is out. His secret is exposed. And his own people have rejected him. When Pharaoh learns of the murder, Moses' life in Egypt is over. The powerful prince, the man "powerful in speech and action," becomes a fugitive. He flees for his life, losing everything in an instant: his status, his family, his wealth, his power, his mission. He runs to the one place where a prince of Egypt has no jurisdiction and no value: the empty, barren wilderness of Midian.

And there, for forty years, he does nothing. He, the man educated in all the wisdom of Egypt, becomes a shepherd. He marries, has a son, and watches another man's sheep. The fire of his youth, the ambition, the self-belief, the confidence in his own power - all of it is slowly baked out of him by the relentless desert sun. The world's "somebody" becomes God's "nobody." The breaking was the making.

The Reluctant Prophet: A Strength that Kneels

The man we meet at the burning bush forty years later is a completely different person. The self-reliant prince is gone, replaced by a humble, hesitant, and broken shepherd. When God calls to him from the fire and commissions him to be the deliverer he once tried to be, Moses' response is not a confident "I'm ready!" It is a series of five profound and revealing objections. These objections are not signs of cowardice; they are the evidence of his newfound meekness. They show a man who has finally learned that he is not enough.

"Who am I?"
(The Crisis of Identity)

His first question is telling: *"Who am I, that I should go to Pharaoh, and that I should bring the sons of Israel out of Egypt?"* Forty years earlier, he knew exactly who he was: a prince of Egypt. Now, he sees himself as a nobody, a forgotten shepherd. His confidence in himself is completely gone.

God's answer is profound. He doesn't build Moses' self-esteem. He doesn't say, "Moses, you're a great guy, you've got this." He completely redirects the basis of Moses' identity. He says,

"Certainly I will be with you." (Exodus 3:12).

The success of the mission has nothing to do with *who you are*, Moses. It has everything to do with *Who is with you*. The meek warrior's confidence is not in himself, but in the presence of his Commander.

2. "What is His name?"
(The Crisis of Authority)

Moses then asks what he should say when the people ask who sent him. He needs to know the source of his authority. He knows his own name carries no weight. God's answer is the foundation of all reality:

"I AM WHO I AM... Say to the sons of Israel, 'I AM has sent me to you.'" (Exodus 3:14).

Moses is being commissioned as an ambassador for the self-existent, eternal God of the universe. His authority is not derived from his resume, but from the One who sent him.

3. "They will not believe me."
(The Crisis of Credibility)

Moses anticipates failure. He remembers the last time he tried to lead, and how his own people rejected him. His past failure has taught him that he has no natural credibility. So God gives him supernatural credibility: the signs of the staff turning into a snake, his hand becoming leprous and then clean. God provides the proof, validating the messenger with His own power.

4. "I am not eloquent."
(The Crisis of Ability)

This is perhaps the most powerful evidence of Moses' transformation. The man who Acts described as "powerful in speech and action" now says, *"Please, Lord, I have never been a man of words... for I am slow of speech and slow of tongue."* He is no longer trusting in his own eloquence or persuasive ability. He is acutely aware of his own weakness. This is the opposite of the proud man who highlights his strengths and hides his flaws. Moses puts his greatest perceived weakness on the table.

God's response is a rebuke wrapped in a reminder:

"Who has made man's mouth? Or who makes him mute or deaf, or seeing or blind? Is it not I, the LORD? Now then go, and I, even I, will be with your mouth, and teach you what you are to say." (Exodus 4:11-12).

God isn't looking for ability; He is looking for availability. He will provide the power.

The forty years in the desert had done their work. They had stripped away the pride of the prince and replaced it with the humility of a man who knew he was utterly dependent on God. This profound sense of his own inadequacy was not his disqualification; it was his ultimate qualification.

The Meek General in Command

This newly forged meekness becomes the source of Moses' incredible strength as a leader. He is powerful precisely because he knows the power is not his own.

When he confronts Pharaoh, he doesn't go as a political negotiator or a military rival. He goes as a messenger. His message is simple, relentless, and bold: "Thus says the LORD, 'Let My people go.'" His courage is not rooted in his own strength, but in the authority of the One who sent him.

But the true test of his meek leadership comes not in the courts of Pharaoh, but in the wilderness with the people he is leading. The Israelites are a difficult, rebellious, and constantly complaining people. A proud leader, a man like Saul, would have crushed their dissent with force or abandoned them in disgust. Moses' meekness allows him to lead in a radically different way.

The ultimate example is the incident of the golden calf. Moses is on Mount Sinai, receiving the Ten Commandments from God. Down below, the people grow impatient and convince Aaron to build them a golden idol to worship. It is an act of profound betrayal and rebellion.

God's anger is white-hot. He says to Moses,

"Now then let Me alone, that My anger may burn against them and that I may destroy them; and I will make of you a great nation." (Exodus 32:10).

Stop and consider this temptation. This is God Himself offering Moses an escape clause. A way out of leading this stiff-necked people. God offers to wipe them out and start over, with Moses as the new patriarch. A proud man, a man fed up with the constant complaining, would have jumped at this. "Finally! I'm rid of them. Let's do it, God. A nation of my own descendants sounds great."

Moses' response is the pinnacle of meek, servant leadership. He doesn't take the offer. Instead, he intercedes. He stands in the gap between a holy God and a sinful people. He doesn't defend their sin; he appeals to God's character. He reminds God of His promises to Abraham, Isaac, and Jacob. He appeals to God's reputation among the nations.

Then, he makes one of the most selfless statements in all of Scripture. He goes back to God and pleads for the people, saying,

"But now, if You will, forgive their sin - and if not, please blot me out from Your book which You have written!" (Exodus 32:32).

This is the heart of a true general. He is willing to be destroyed for the sake of his mutinous troops. He so identifies with his people that he would rather be destroyed with them than saved without them. This is not the act of a weak or passive man. This is an act of ferocious, courageous, and selfless love - a strength that is only born from true meekness.

Time and again, when the people rebel or when his leadership is challenged by his own family, Moses' first response is not to defend himself or to lash out. His default posture is to fall on his face before God. He doesn't need to win arguments because he knows God is his vindicator. He leads from his knees.

The boy who was raised a prince had to become a shepherd to learn humility. The man who thought his own strength was enough had to be broken by failure to learn dependence. Moses' life teaches the spiritual warrior the most vital of all lessons: God's power is perfected in weakness. The strongest leader is not the one with the most impressive resume, but the one in constant, selfless prayer. He was the meekest man on earth, and for that very reason, he was one of the most powerful leaders in history.

Shane W. Cunningham

Chapter 9
Paul: The Tamed Revolutionary

*"The tamed lion has the strength to
make himself small, to enter another's
world, in order to bring them to the King."*

OUR GALLERY OF spiritual warriors would be incomplete without its most explosive and dynamic figure. He was a man who possessed no throne, commanded no army, and held no formal office of worldly power. And yet, his impact on human history arguably eclipses that of every king and general we have studied. He was a man of pure, uncut intensity. His intellect was a weapon, his passion a wildfire, and his will a force of nature.

We are speaking, of course, of the Apostle Paul.

His life poses a crucial question for our investigation. What does meekness look like in a man who is, by every natural measure, the opposite of mild? What happens when a human dynamo, a man of ferocious zeal and absolute conviction, is brought to his knees? Does God extinguish the fire to make him useful? Or does He simply seize control of the blaze and aim it at a new target?

The life of Paul provides a clear and stunning answer. The man we meet as Saul of Tarsus is an untamed lion, a revolutionary spirit convinced of his own righteousness and dedicated to destroying his enemies. The man who dies as Paul the Apostle is a tamed lion, a revolutionary spirit who has willingly placed his own ferocious will on a leash held by the hand of Jesus Christ. His conversion did not make him a weaker man; it made him a submitted one. And in that submission, he found a power that would change the world. Paul's life is the final, definitive proof that meekness is not the absence of strength, but the harnessing of it for a mission far greater than oneself.

Saul of Tarsus: The Untamed Lion

To appreciate the miracle of Paul's transformation, we must first have an honest look at the man he was before. It is a profound mistake to see the pre-Christian Saul as simply a "bad guy." In his own mind, and in the minds of his peers, he was the best of the best. He was the hero of his own story. He was a man utterly convinced that he was doing the work of God.

First, consider his pedigree. This was not an uneducated gangster. Paul himself, later in life, lays out his perfect resume:

"Circumcised the eighth day, of the nation of Israel, of the tribe of Benjamin, a Hebrew of Hebrews; as to the Law, a Pharisee; as to zeal, a persecutor of the church; as to the righteousness which is in the Law, found blameless." (Philippians 3:5-6).

He was a man at the absolute apex of his culture. A Pharisee, the most respected and rigorously devout sect of Judaism. He was trained in Jerusalem under Gamaliel, the most celebrated rabbi of his generation. His knowledge of the Scriptures would have been comprehensive. His intellect was razor-sharp. He was, by every religious and academic metric of his day, an A+ student.

But his defining characteristic, by his own admission, was zeal. The Greek word is *zelos*, and it doesn't mean mild enthusiasm. It means a searing, consuming, and often violent passion. Saul looked at the fledgling Christian movement, this new sect that claimed a crucified carpenter was the divine Messiah, and he saw it as a blasphemous, cancerous heresy. In his mind, these "followers of the Way" were a threat to the purity of his faith, the integrity of his nation, and the very honor of God. And like any zealous revolutionary, he believed it was his sacred duty to stamp it out.

His zeal was not merely academic. He was a man of terrifying action. The book of Acts introduces him at the stoning of Stephen, the first Christian martyr, "consenting to his death." But he doesn't stop there. We are told that Saul began to "ravage the church." The word in Greek suggests a wild animal tearing its prey apart. Then comes one of the most chilling descriptions of a man's inner state in all of Scripture: he was

"Breathing threats and murder against the disciples of the Lord." (Acts 9:1).

This was his oxygen. He went to the high priest and obtained official letters, a government sanction, to hunt these people down. He planned to go to Damascus, drag Christian men and women from their homes, and bring them back to Jerusalem in chains.

This is the man we must see clearly. A brilliant, highly educated, morally upright, and religiously passionate man who was utterly convinced of his own righteousness. He was armed with institutional power and fueled by a relentless, violent passion. He was an untamed lion, hunting the people of God. He was the monster, and he believed he was the hero.

The Damascus Road: The Taming

How do you stop a man like Saul? You don't persuade him with a clever argument; his mind is too well-fortified. You don't appeal to his compassion; his zeal has burned it away. You don't intimidate him with a threat; he is the one who breathes out threats.

A man like Saul can only be stopped by an overwhelming, undeniable, and superior display of power. And that is exactly what happened on the road to Damascus.

As he traveled, a light from heaven, brighter than the midday sun, flashed around him. It threw him from his horse and pinned him to the earth. A voice from the sky called him by name, a voice of immense power and profound intimacy:

"Saul, Saul, why are you persecuting Me?"(Acts 9:4)

This was not a negotiation. It was a takedown. God did not reason with Saul's intellect; He completely overrode his senses. He did not ask for permission to enter Saul's life; He invaded it. He met Saul on the only terms a man like Saul would understand: absolute power.

Saul, the great inquisitor, is reduced to asking two simple, terrified questions. "Who are you, Lord?" And, "What do you want me to do?" In a single moment, the hunter becomes the captive.

Then comes the masterstroke of his taming. The voice identifies Himself:

"I am Jesus, whom you are persecuting." (Acts 9:5)

In that instant, Saul's entire worldview, his entire life's mission, is not just proven wrong; it is revealed to be a direct assault on the very God he claimed to serve. The cancer he thought he was fighting was, in fact, the body of the living God. It is an ego-shattering, soul-crushing revelation.

Saul is left blind. For three days, he is in a world of total darkness. Think of the significance of this. The man who saw the world in the black-and-white clarity of his own righteousness is now unable to see anything at all. The man of action is now helpless, having to be led by the hand into the city like a child. His mission is aborted. His power is gone. His authority is meaningless. In the silent darkness, unable to eat or drink, the proud Pharisee is systematically dismantled. The untamed lion is caged, broken, and humbled. It is the most important and agonizing three days of his life.

His healing comes at the hands of a man named Ananias, a simple disciple in Damascus. Ananias is, by Saul's own standards, a nobody. He is one of the very people Saul came to arrest. And now, this proud, brilliant man must wait in darkness until this humble follower of the Way comes and, by the grace of the God he once hated, restores his sight. The humiliation is total. The taming is complete.

Paul the Apostle: The Lion on a Leash

The man who rises from this experience is not a weaker Saul. He is a new creation named Paul. The fire of his personality has not been extinguished; it has been placed in a new furnace. The engine of his zeal has not been scrapped; it has been dropped into a new chassis and aimed in a new direction. God didn't want a less passionate Paul. He wanted a captured Paul.

The rest of Paul's life is a demonstration of what this harnessed power looks like.

His Intellect Was Redirected

The same brilliant mind that once constructed intricate legalistic arguments against the followers of Jesus is now used to construct the most profound and powerful theological arguments for the gospel of Jesus Christ. He takes his encyclopedic knowledge of the Old Testament and shows how it all points to Jesus. He writes the letters that will become the bedrock of Christian theology for the next two millennia. The intellectual firepower is the same, but it's now aimed at building the very church he once tried to destroy.

His Passion Was Refocused

The same fiery passion that drove him to persecute Christians now drives him to suffer for them. His missionary journeys are a testament to his relentless, unstoppable drive. He is a man on a mission from God, and nothing will stand in his way. Read the list of what he endured:

"Five times I received from the Jews thirty-nine lashes. Three times I was beaten with rods, once I was stoned, three times I was shipwrecked, a night and a day I have spent in the deep." (2 Corinthians 11:24-25).

He faced constant danger, betrayal, hunger, and hardship. The man who once breathed threats and murder now endured threats and murder, all for the sake of the gospel. The intensity is identical; the object of that intensity has been completely transformed.

His Power Was Redefined

This is the very core of his newfound meekness. In his old life, Saul's power came from his heritage, his education, his position, and his own ferocious will. In his new life, Paul discovers a paradoxical secret: true spiritual power flows from the admission of weakness.

This lesson is solidified in his experience with the "thorn in the flesh." He describes some kind of chronic, tormenting affliction. This man, this spiritual giant who had been given heavenly visions, pleaded with God three times to take it away. The answer he received became the central operating principle of his life:

"My grace is sufficient for you, for power is perfected in weakness." (2 Corinthians 12:9).

This is a revolutionary concept. God is not looking for our strength, our talent, or our self-sufficiency. He is looking for our weakness, because our weakness is the empty vessel into which He can pour His power. A proud man cannot accept this. A proud man hides his weakness and highlights his strength. But the meek warrior, the tamed lion, does the opposite. Paul's response is the battle cry of the truly meek:

"Most gladly, therefore, I will rather boast about my weaknesses, so that the power of Christ may dwell in me" (2 Corinthians 12:9).

This redefinition of power allowed Paul to do something the proud Saul could never have contemplated: he made himself adaptable for the sake of the mission. The rigid Pharisee who defined himself by separation from anything unclean now makes one of the most stunning statements of meekness in the Bible:

"To the Jews I became as a Jew, in order to win Jews... to those who are without law, as without law... to the weak I

became weak, that I might win the weak; I have become all things to all men, so that I may by all means save some." (1 Corinthians 9:20-22).

This is not the statement of a people-pleaser. This is the strategic adaptability of a warrior who has died to his own ego. It requires immense strength of character to lay aside your personal preferences, your cultural comforts, and your individual "rights" for the sake of reaching someone else. A weak man, an insecure man, cannot do this; his identity is too fragile. Only a truly strong man, a man whose identity is securely anchored in Christ, can become this flexible.

The untamed lion roars to defend his own territory. The tamed lion has the strength to make himself small, to enter another's world, in order to bring them to the King.

Finally, we see Paul's meekness in his fatherly heart. This is the same man who could write a letter like Galatians, a blistering, fierce, no-holds-barred takedown of false teaching. He never lost his roar. But he could also write to the Thessalonian church and say,

"We were gentle among you, as a nursing mother tenderly cares for her own children." (1 Thessalonians 2:7).

He could plead with a runaway slave's owner, Philemon, not with orders, but with a gentle appeal based on love. He knew when to fight and when to nurture. He knew when to unleash his apostolic authority and when to set it aside. This ability to modulate his immense personal power based on the needs of the mission and the people he served is the final, compelling evidence of a lion on a leash.

Paul's journey is a staggering testament. He began as a man defined by his own strength, his own intellect, and his own zeal. He was the perfect specimen of self-righteous power. On the road to Damascus, a stronger Lion met him, broke him, and brought him to heel. The rest of his life was the result of that beautiful, violent surrender. God did not break Paul's spirit; He captured it. He took the most dangerous revolutionary of his day and made him His own.

And in doing so, He proved for all time that meekness is not about becoming less of who you are. It's about submitting all that you are—your passion, your drive, your intellect, and your strength—to the loving command of a greater King.

Shane W. Cunningham

Chapter 10
The Home Front:
Leading with Gentle Strength

"He is obsessed with the appearance of respect, but he has no idea how to cultivate the reality of it."

FOR GENERATIONS, MEN have been taught to view their home as a castle. It's a place of refuge after a long day of fighting battles in the world. It's a place to rest, to recharge, to be the king. And while there's a sliver of truth in that, it's a dangerously incomplete picture. A spiritual warrior must understand a more profound truth: the home is not a refuge *from* the battle; it is the *primary* battlefield.

It is the command post. It is the proving ground. It is the single most important leadership assignment a man will ever receive from God. The character, discipline, and strength forged in the secret place of a man's family life will determine his effectiveness in every other arena. You cannot be a lion in the boardroom and a lamb at the breakfast table and call that integrity. Your truest self is the man you are when only your wife and children are watching.

This is the place where our entire investigation into meekness moves from the theoretical to the intensely practical. It's easy to admire the restrained strength of David in a cave or the selfless intercession of Moses on a mountain. It is another thing entirely to practice that same restrained, selfless strength when your three-year-old has just drawn on the wall with a permanent marker, your teenager is challenging your authority, and you and your wife are disagreeing on finances for the third time this week.

The world offers two primary models of leadership for a man in his home, and both are catastrophic failures. One is the tyrant; the other is the abdicator. One is an abuse of power; the other is a desertion of duty. The meek warrior, the man who follows the command of Jesus Christ, must reject both of these broken models and forge a third path. It is the path of gentle strength, of power under perfect control, deployed for the flourishing of those under his care.

The Broken Models: The Tyrant and The Abdicator

Before we can build the right command structure, we must demolish the faulty ones that our culture and our own sinful hearts are so quick to construct.

1. The Tyrant: The Brittle Strength of Saul

The tyrant is the man who mistakes control for leadership. He runs his home like a drill sergeant runs a barracks. His word is law, not because it is wise or loving, but simply because it is his. He leads through intimidation, anger, and a rigid, unyielding set of rules. His family may comply with his demands, but they do so out of fear, not out of love or respect. There is no joy in his home, only a tense, fragile order.

This is the leadership model of King Saul. It is a strength built on ego and insecurity. The tyrant shouts because he is terrified of being seen as weak. He demands unquestioning obedience because he cannot handle his authority being challenged. He is obsessed with the *appearance* of respect, but he has no idea how to cultivate the *reality* of it. He may have a quiet home, but it is the quiet of a battlefield after a brutal defeat, not the quiet of a peaceful harbor.

This is not strength. It is brittle. Like Saul, the man who leads this way will eventually shatter under pressure, because his family will not rally to him in a crisis. They will simply try to stay out of the shrapnel zone. A man who uses his physical, emotional, or spiritual power to dominate his family is not a leader; he is a bully. And he is profoundly failing his mission.

2. The Abdicator: The Weakness of the "Nice Guy"

On the other end of the spectrum is the man who, often in a well-intentioned effort to avoid being a tyrant, gives up his leadership role entirely. He is the passive man, the conflict-avoidant "nice guy." He wants peace at any price, and he is willing to sacrifice his God-given responsibility to get it.

He doesn't lead; he placates. He doesn't set a direction for his family; he just goes with the flow. He outsources the difficult job of discipline to his wife. He avoids tough conversations. He retreats into his hobbies, his work, or his phone, leaving a vacuum of leadership at the center of his home. His wife is left feeling like a single mother, and his children are left without a firm, loving standard to guide them. The home may not be overtly oppressive, but it is chaotic, drifting without a rudder.

This is not meekness; it is pathetic weakness. It is a soldier deserting his post under fire. It is a failure of courage. The abdicator may think he is being gentle, but his passivity is a selfish act that leaves his family exposed and vulnerable. He has traded his sacred duty for a quiet life, and the cost of that trade is the spiritual and emotional health of the people he is called to protect.

Both of these models are rooted in fear. The tyrant fears losing control. The abdicator fears facing conflict. The meek warrior is called to a higher standard, a leadership model rooted not in fear, but in love and sacrifice.

The Warrior's Mandate: To Love as Christ Loved

For the Christian man, the mission brief for family leadership is not found in a corporate leadership seminar or a self-help book. It is found in one of the most challenging and beautiful passages in all of Scripture. The Apostle Paul lays out the command in stunningly clear terms:

"Husbands, love your wives, just as Christ also loved the church and gave Himself up for her." (Ephesians 5:25).

This single verse obliterates both the tyrant and the abdicator. This is our mandate. This is the entire strategy. Notice what it does *not* say. It does not say, "Husbands, be the boss of your wives." It does not say, "Husbands, make sure your wives submit to you." It places the entire weight of responsibility, the entire burden of action, squarely on the husband's shoulders. Our command is not to rule, but to love. And the definition of that love is the most radical and selfless standard imaginable: the love of Jesus for His people.

How did Christ love the church? He gave Himself up for her. This is the essence of meek leadership. It is the voluntary laying down of your own power, your own preferences, your own rights, and your own ego for the good of the one you are leading. It is a daily dying to self. A good military officer eats last. A true spiritual warrior places the needs of his family ahead of his own.

This kind of love is the ultimate expression of power under control. It requires immense strength. It is easy to be a tyrant; all you need is a loud voice and a selfish heart. It is easy to be an abdicator; all you need is a weak will. But to love your wife as Christ loved the church requires the strength of a man who is secure in his identity, submitted to God, and committed to a mission far greater than his own comfort.

Tactics for Leading Your Wife with Gentle Strength

This Christ-like love isn't just a feeling; it's a series of tactical decisions. It is love in action.

The Strength to Listen: A tyrant lectures; a meek warrior listens. And listening is not merely the absence of talking. It is an active, engaged, and humble act. It is the willingness to enter her world, to understand her perspective, and to value her heart above your need to be right. When your wife is talking, your mission is not to formulate your rebuttal. Your mission is to understand. Ask questions. Make eye contact. Put down your phone. This simple act communicates value and honor more powerfully than a thousand flowery words.

The Strength to Serve: Christ demonstrated his leadership by washing his disciples' feet. A meek warrior leads his wife by serving her. This means looking for ways to lighten her load without being asked. It means doing the dishes, helping with the laundry, taking on the bedtime routine with the kids. These are not "chores" that you "help" with; they are your shared responsibility. Every act of service is a deposit in the bank of her heart (her Love Bank), a tangible demonstration that your strength is *for* her, not *against* her. A man who is too proud to serve his wife is too small to lead her.

The Strength to Validate, Not Just Solve: Men are hardwired to be fixers. When our wife comes to us with a problem or a frustration, our immediate instinct is to jump in with a ten-point plan to solve it. But often, she is not looking for a solution. She is looking for a partner. She needs to know that you hear her, that you understand her frustration, and that you are on her team. A meek warrior has the self-control to restrain his inner "Mr. Fix-It" and simply offer empathy. A simple phrase like, "Wow, that sounds incredibly frustrating. I'm so sorry you had to deal with that today," is often more powerful than any solution you could offer. First connect, then (if she asks) you can conquer the problem together.

The Strength to Ask for Forgiveness: This may be the ultimate tactical advantage of the meek warrior. A tyrant cannot apologize because his ego is too fragile. An abdicator avoids conflict, so he never has to. But a man who is truly strong, whose identity is secure in Christ, is not afraid to admit when he is wrong. Saying a genuine, no-excuses "I was wrong. I sinned against you. Will you please forgive me?" is one of the most powerful and healing things a husband can do. It models humility, dismantles pride, and creates a culture of grace in your marriage.

Tactics for Leading Your Children:
The Father as a Discipler

The warrior's mandate extends to his children. Paul is again crystal clear on the mission:

"Fathers, do not provoke your children to anger, but bring them up in the discipline and instruction of the Lord." (Ephesians 6:4).

This command has two parts, like a perfectly balanced weapon. It requires both a gentle hand and a firm hand.

The Gentle Hand: "Do Not Provoke"

A father has immense power in the life of his child. He can use that power to build or to crush. Paul warns us not to use our power in a way that "provokes" or "exasperates" our children, crushing their spirit. What does this look like?

Hypocrisy: Demanding a standard of them that you do not live by yourself.

Inconsistency: Enforcing rules one day and ignoring them the next, creating a chaotic and confusing environment.

Unrealistic Expectations: Demanding perfection and offering constant criticism, making them feel they can never measure up.

Harshness: Using discipline as an outlet for your own anger and frustration, rather than as a tool for their instruction.

A meek warrior has his own power under control. He is patient, he is consistent, and his default posture toward his children is one of encouragement, not criticism.

The Firm Hand: "Discipline and Instruction"

Gentleness does not mean a lack of discipline. The command is also to bring them up in the *discipline* and *instruction* of the Lord. It's crucial to understand the difference between punishment and discipline. Punishment is backward-looking; it's about paying a penalty for a *past* wrong. Discipline is forward-looking; it's about training for *future* character.

The Greek word for discipline here is *paideia*, which is about nurturing, training, and education. A meek warrior-father disciplines with a clear objective: to forge a child's character, to teach them wisdom, and to point them toward Jesus. His discipline is firm, consistent, and always administered in love, not in anger. He is like a master craftsman shaping a precious piece of work. The pressure must be firm enough to shape, but gentle enough not to break.

Ultimately, the most powerful tool of discipline and instruction is a father's engaged presence. It is easy to provide for your children financially. It is much harder to be truly present with them emotionally and spiritually. To put down your work, turn off the TV, and get on the floor to play with them. To ask them about their day and actually listen to the answer. To pray with them and for them. Your life is the textbook from which they will learn what it means to be a man, a husband, a father, and a follower of Christ.

The Legacy of a Gentle Warrior

The world will tell you to measure your life by the size of your paycheck, the title on your business card, or the square footage of your house. God has a different metric. The truest measure of a man's strength is the health and vitality of his home.

Leading your family with meekness is the most difficult, and the most rewarding, mission you will ever undertake. It will require more courage than facing an enemy on the battlefield and more wisdom than navigating a corporate negotiation. It will require you to die to yourself daily, to admit when you are wrong, to serve when you would rather be served, and to love when you feel unloved.

But the legacy of a man who leads this way is eternal. It is a wife who feels safe, cherished, and honored. It is children who grow up knowing the firm but gentle love of their earthly father, making it easier for them to understand the love of their Heavenly Father. This is the legacy of a warrior who understood that the most important ground to defend was the ground within his own four walls.

Shane W. Cunningham

Chapter 11
The Workplace:
The Quiet Professional

---

*"The quiet professional is secure
in his identity in Christ, so he is
free to simply do the work."*

AFTER THE FINAL prayer has been said over the dinner table and the last child has been tucked into bed, the spiritual warrior's mission is not over. The next morning, it simply shifts to a new theater of operations: the workplace.

This is a different kind of battlefield. The weapons are not swords and spears, but spreadsheets and presentations. The skirmishes are fought in conference rooms and email chains. But make no mistake, it is a battle. It is a battle for integrity, a battle for character, and a battle for influence. The modern workplace, with its relentless focus on profit, promotion, and personal branding, is a culture-building machine. And the culture it most often builds is one of pride, fear, and self-preservation.

Into this environment walks the man committed to meekness. How does he survive? More than that, how does he lead? How does he pursue excellence and ambition without selling his soul to the corporate machine? The world tells him he must be a shark, a ruthless closer, a political animal. The gospel calls him to be something far more powerful. It calls him to be a quiet professional.

The term "quiet professional" is borrowed from the world of elite special operations. It describes a warrior who is defined not by how loudly he talks, but by how skillfully he executes the mission. His reputation is built on competence, not charisma. He is disciplined, adaptable, and utterly reliable. He doesn't need to broadcast his accomplishments because his results speak for themselves. He is a master of his craft, a man of unshakable character who puts the mission and his team before his own ego.

This is a perfect, modern-day picture of the meek warrior in a professional setting. He is a man of immense capability, a monster at his craft, who has placed his strength under the complete control of a higher calling. He stands in stark contrast to the two broken models of professional success that dominate our culture.

The Broken Models:
The Politician and The Bulldozer

Walk into almost any office, factory, or job site, and you will find men striving for success by following one of two flawed playbooks.

1. The Political Operator: The Treachery of Absalom

The political operator is the master of perception. His primary skill is not the work itself, but the management of his image. He is an expert at "managing up," ensuring that his superiors see him as indispensable, agreeable, and brilliant. He is a master of the meeting, speaking just enough to sound insightful without ever taking a real risk. He is quick to attach his name to a successful project and just as quick to find a scapegoat when things go wrong.

His loyalty is not to the company or to his team, but only to himself. He builds alliances based on mutual benefit and discards them when they are no longer useful. He is smooth, charming, and he is often deeply untrustworthy. His playbook is not one of creating value, but of capturing credit.

He is the modern-day Absalom, the son of King David who stood at the city gates, stole the hearts of the people with smooth words, and used that influence to launch a treacherous coup against his own father. The political operator builds his career on the shaky ground of perception and manipulation. He may rise high, but his foundation is rotten.

2. The Bulldozer: The Brittle Strength of Saul

The bulldozer, on the other hand, often scoffs at the politician. The bulldozer is all about results. He is aggressive, driven, and demanding. He gets things done. But he does so with a trail of human carnage in his wake. He is the boss who rules by fear, the colleague who will run you over to win an argument, the salesman who will say anything to close a deal.

He mistakes aggression for strength and intimidation for leadership. He often produces short-term results, but he creates a toxic culture of fear and burnout. People do not follow him out of loyalty; they obey him out of a desire to avoid his wrath. Like the politician, his ultimate motivation is his own ego. He needs to win, to be seen as the smartest and toughest person in the room, to prove his own value.

He is a modern-day King Saul. He may look the part of a powerful leader, but underneath the bluster is a deep insecurity. He is terrified of failure and threatened by the success of others. His strength is loud, obnoxious, and ultimately brittle. A team led by a bulldozer will eventually break, because fear is a poor long-term motivator.

The meek warrior rejects both of these paths. He is not a conniving politician, and he is not a belligerent bulldozer. His path is one of quiet, disciplined excellence, rooted in a completely different understanding of the purpose of his work.

The Quiet Professional's Mandate: An Audience of One

The central operating principle for the meek warrior in the workplace is found in a simple command from the Apostle Paul to a church in a small, working-class town:

"Whatever you do, do your work heartily, as for the Lord rather than for men." (Colossians 3:23).

This single verse fundamentally changes everything. It reassigns our ultimate boss. It reframes our motivation. It redefines our standard of success. The quiet professional understands that while he may have a human supervisor who signs his paychecks, he ultimately works for an audience of One. His true performance review will be given by the King of Kings.

This perspective is incredibly liberating. It frees a man from the soul-crushing need to please everyone around him. It frees him from the hamster wheel of office politics. It frees him from the fear of a difficult boss or a toxic colleague. His identity is not tied to his job title. His value is not determined by his last quarterly review. He has been given an assignment by his true Commander, and his mission is to execute that assignment with excellence, as an act of worship.

This is the source of his quiet confidence. The politician is insecure, so he must constantly manage his image. The bulldozer is insecure, so he must constantly prove his strength. The quiet professional is secure in his identity in Christ, so he is free to simply do the work.

The Ammunition of Excellence

The primary weapon of the quiet professional is not a silver tongue or a ruthless demeanor. It is world-class competence. His goal is to be so good at his job that his work speaks for itself. He doesn't need to play political games because the value he creates is undeniable.

The phrase "do your work heartily" in Colossians 3:23 comes from a Greek phrase that means "out of the soul." It implies a deep, passionate, and all-in commitment. The meek warrior does not give a half-hearted effort. He is not a slacker. He does not cut corners. Whether he is a CEO, a plumber, a teacher, or a janitor, he approaches his work with the mindset of a master craftsman.

He pursues excellence for two reasons. First, it is an act of worship. The carpenter who builds a sturdy, beautiful cabinet is offering a prayer with his hands. The accountant who prepares a meticulous, honest financial statement is offering a sacrifice of integrity. Doing our work well brings glory to the God who created us to work, to build, to solve, and to create.

Second, excellence is the foundation of our influence. Nobody listens to the advice of an incompetent fool. A man who is lazy, unreliable, or sloppy in his work has no platform from which to speak. But a man who is known for his skill, his integrity, and his reliability earns the respect of his colleagues. When a crisis hits, people don't turn to the smooth-talking politician or the loud-mouthed bulldozer. They turn to the quiet professional who they know can get the job done. Competence is the currency of trust.

This requires a commitment to lifelong learning and a humble, teachable spirit. The quiet professional is always sharpening his skills, reading, studying, and seeking to improve his craft. He rejects the prideful notion that he has "arrived" and embraces the humble posture of a student.

The Tactical Field Manual

With this foundation of working for an audience of One and a commitment to excellence, the quiet professional employs a set of tactics that are radically different from the world's.

1. The Strength to Speak Last

In most meetings, the first person to speak is often trying to establish dominance or prove their intelligence. The quiet professional has nothing to prove. He practices the discipline of listening. He gathers intelligence. He seeks to understand the different perspectives in the room. He watches the dynamics at play. He waits. It is only after he has a full understanding of the situation that he offers his contribution. Because he has not wasted his breath on posturing, his words, when they come, are often more thoughtful, more strategic, and carry far more weight. This is not passivity; it is tactical patience.

2. The Strength to Give Away Credit

A proud man, a man like Saul, hoards credit. He needs the spotlight to feed his insecure ego. When a project succeeds, he makes sure everyone knows it was his idea. The quiet professional, a man whose confidence is in Christ, has the strength to do the opposite. He actively looks for opportunities to deflect praise and to highlight the contributions of his teammates. He understands that his mission is the success of the team, not the advancement of his own career. A leader who gives away credit builds a fiercely loyal and motivated team. It is a profound display of confidence. He is not threatened by the success of others; he celebrates it.

3. The Strength to Own the Blame

This is the acid test of a leader. When a mistake is made, when a project fails, where does the finger point? The political operator has a scapegoat ready. The bulldozer will throw his team under the bus. The quiet professional, especially if he is in a position of leadership, takes the hit. He stands before his superiors and says, "The buck stops with me. I am responsible, and here is my plan to fix it." This act of courage and integrity builds a level of trust that is almost unbreakable. His team knows that he has their back, and they will go to war for a leader like that.

4. The Strength to Do the Thankless Job

The quiet professional is not above any task that serves the mission. He is the one who volunteers for the difficult assignment that no one else wants. He is the one who stays late to help a colleague meet a deadline. He is the one who does the unglamorous, unseen work that is necessary for the team to succeed. This is the corporate equivalent of Jesus washing his disciples' feet. A man who is too important to do the small jobs is too small to be trusted with the big ones. This servant-hearted approach is a powerful, counter-cultural testimony in a world where everyone is jockeying for the high-profile assignments.

A Different Definition of Success

The world will try to force you into its mold. It will pressure you to become a politician or a bulldozer. It will tell you that meekness is weakness and that you have to look out for number one.

The quiet professional understands that he is playing a different game with a different scoreboard. The world defines success by a man's title, the size of his office, and the number of people who report to him. The meek warrior defines success by his faithfulness to his true Commander.

His goal is not simply to climb the ladder, but to be a faithful ambassador of the Kingdom in whatever cubicle, corner office, or construction site he has been placed. His excellence, his integrity, his calm under pressure, and his servant's heart are his testimony. He is a quiet professional, and his work is an act of worship, performed before an audience of One.

Chapter 12
Absorbing the Hit:
The Strength to Suffer Wrongly

"A man who can absorb a hit without retaliating is a man who cannot be controlled."

IT HAPPENS IN A flash. It's a passive-aggressive comment from a coworker in a meeting, designed to subtly undermine your credibility. It's a false accusation from a family member that twists your motives into something ugly. It's a string of venomous comments on a social media post you made. It's the sting of betrayal from a friend who shares a confidence.

It is a direct hit.

In that instant, a thousand alarms go off in your soul. Your heart rate quickens. Your face flushes with heat. A primal, powerful, and deeply human instinct takes over. *Fight or flight*. Defend. Justify. Explain. And above all, retaliate. Your mind races, formulating the perfect, cutting rebuttal. Your pride, wounded and bleeding, screams for vindication. It demands that you hit back, harder, to put the attacker back in their place and re-establish your honor.

This is the warrior's instinct. It is the law of the jungle and the law of the schoolyard. An eye for an eye. A tooth for a tooth. An insult for an insult.

But the spiritual warrior is called to a higher law, a more difficult and disciplined way of fighting. He is called to master the art of absorbing the hit. This is not weakness. It is not cowardice. It is, perhaps, the single greatest display of a man's strength. It is the supernatural ability to take the full force of an opponent's hatred, malice, or ignorance and refuse to be poisoned by it. It is the spiritual jiu-jitsu of using the energy of your enemy's attack not to fuel your own rage, but to expose their weakness and demonstrate your Christ-like self-control.

A man who can absorb a hit without retaliating is a man who cannot be controlled. His peace is not dependent on the approval of others. His identity is not up for negotiation. He is truly free, and he is truly dangerous to the kingdom of darkness.

The Broken Models:
The Porcupine and The Doormat

Just as in every other area of life, the world offers us two broken, ineffective ways to handle being wronged. Both are rooted in fear and lead to failure.

1. The Porcupine: Every Hill is a Hill to Die On

The porcupine is the man who is perpetually on the defensive. His quills are always up. He interprets every question as an attack, every criticism as a declaration of war. He is argumentative, easily offended, and obsessed with being right. When he takes a hit, however small, he doesn't just return fire; he empties the entire magazine. He escalates minor disagreements into major conflicts. He burns bridges over trivial matters.

We all know this man. He's the guy who clogs up your email inbox with a 12-paragraph defense of a minor decision. He's the guy on Facebook who will argue with a stranger for three days over a political meme. His life is a series of exhausting, never-ending battles for his own honor.

But this isn't strength; it's a symptom of profound insecurity. The porcupine's ego is so fragile that it cannot withstand the slightest challenge. Like King Saul, he is terrified of being seen as weak or foolish, and so he overcompensates with aggression. He may win the argument, but he loses respect. He may get the last word, but he loses his relationships. He is a slave to the opinions of others, because he has given them the power to control his emotional state with a single critical word.

2. The Doormat: Suffering as a Sign of Weakness

On the other side is the doormat. This is the man who suffers wrongly, but not out of strength. He endures insults and disrespect out of a fear of conflict. He is the classic passive aggressive. He won't stand up for himself, but he will store away the hurt, letting it curdle into a quiet, simmering bitterness. He may appear to be "turning the other cheek," but he is not making a conscious, powerful choice. He is simply surrendering out of weakness.

His silence is not the disciplined calm of a warrior; it is the fearful silence of a victim. By never pushing back, by never speaking the truth in love, he enables the bad behavior of others. His passivity is not a virtue; it is a failure of courage that harms both himself and the person wronging him. This is not meekness. It is the abandonment of a man's responsibility to stand for what is right, even when it's uncomfortable.

The meek warrior rejects both paths. He is not an aggressive porcupine, and he is not a passive doormat. His response is something else entirely: a conscious, strategic, and powerful choice to absorb the hit for the sake of a greater mission.

The Warrior's Mandate: The Standard of the Slapped Cheek

The mission orders for this kind of engagement come directly from Jesus Christ, and they are among the most radical and challenging words ever spoken:

"But I say to you, do not resist an evil person; but whoever slaps you on your right cheek, turn the other to him also." (Matthew 5:39).

For two thousand years, this verse has been misinterpreted as a call to be a doormat, to enable abuse, and to surrender in the face of evil. This is a profound misunderstanding of the cultural context and the spiritual genius of Jesus' command.

In the first-century world, a slap on the right cheek from a right-handed person was not a punch. It was a backhand. A punch was a blow between equals, a challenge to a fight. A backhand was an insult. It was what a master did to a slave, a Roman did to a Jew. It was a gesture of utter contempt, designed to humiliate, to put you in your place, to remind you that you are an inferior.

So, when Jesus says to turn the other cheek, He is not saying, "Let them beat you senseless." He is giving a radical strategy for seizing the moral high ground. By turning your left cheek, you are presenting a target for a punch, a blow between equals. You are silently and powerfully communicating: "Your attempt to humiliate me has failed. You can treat me as an inferior, but I refuse to accept that role. My dignity is not in your hands. I am a human being, made in the image of God, and I demand to be treated as such. Now, what will you do?"

It is a stunning act of non-violent defiance. It breaks the cycle of insult and retaliation. It exposes the ugliness of the aggressor's action and forces them to make a choice. It is the exact opposite of being a doormat. It is a conscious, courageous, and deeply meek act of war against the spirit of pride and humiliation.

Case Study: David and the Man Who Threw Rocks

If we need a living example of this principle in action, we need look no further than King David, at the lowest moment of his life. He is fleeing Jerusalem, a king in exile, betrayed by his own son Absalom who has seized the throne. His power is gone, his kingdom is lost, and his life hangs by a thread.

As he and his small band of loyal men are walking, a man named Shimei, from the clan of the fallen King Saul, comes out and begins to publicly humiliate him. He throws stones at the king. He kicks up dust. And he screams curses:

"Get out, get out, you man of bloodshed, and worthless fellow! The LORD has returned upon you all the bloodshed of the house of Saul... and behold, you are ruined for your own evil, because you are a man of bloodshed!" (2 Samuel 16:7-8).

This is the ultimate insult. It is a total, public, and vicious attack on David's character and his kingship.

At David's side is his nephew, Abishai, one of his fiercest and most loyal generals. Abishai is a porcupine, a man of action. He sees the hit, and his immediate instinct is to retaliate with overwhelming force. He says to David,

"Why should this dead dog curse my lord the king? Let me go over now and take off his head." (2 Samuel 16:9).

This is the logical, worldly response. It is the response of any warrior who sees his commander being dishonored. Punish the insubordination. Eliminate the threat. Defend the king's honor.

David's response exemplifies meekness. He stops his general. He absorbs the hit completely. His reply reveals the heart of a man whose focus is not on his own honor, but on the sovereignty of God. He says,

"Let him alone and let him curse, for the LORD has told him. Perhaps the LORD will look on my affliction and return good to me for his cursing today" (2 Samuel 16:12).

Stop and analyze the profound strength in this moment.

He sees God's hand. David doesn't see Shimei as the ultimate source of his pain. He has the spiritual vision to see that God may be using this humiliating experience for a purpose. His focus is vertical.

He trusts God's justice. He doesn't need Abishai to be his vindicator because he trusts that God will ultimately settle the accounts. He is willing to wait for God's justice, which is far more perfect than man's revenge.

His identity is secure. A lesser king, an insecure man like Saul, would have been forced to kill Shimei to save face. He would have seen the insult as a threat to his authority. But David, even in this broken state, is secure enough in his identity as God's chosen that he can endure the cursing of a "dead dog." He has nothing to prove.

David absorbs the rocks, the dust, and the curses, and he just keeps walking. This is not the act of a weak king. It is the act of a king whose strength is so deep that the petty attacks of his enemies cannot touch his soul.

The Tactical Field Manual: How to Absorb the Hit

This kind of response does not come naturally. It must be trained. It is a spiritual muscle that must be developed through disciplined practice.

Tactic 1: The Sacred Pause. When the insult comes, your first move is to do nothing. Do not speak. Do not type. Do not react. Breathe. Create a two-second gap between the stimulus and your response. This tiny pause is a "holy space". It is just enough time for the Holy Spirit to step in and intercept the signal from your screaming flesh. It is the moment you choose discipline over instinct.

Tactic 2: Reframe the Enemy. In that sacred pause, recognize who your real enemy is. It is not your coworker, your spouse, or the anonymous troll online. Your true enemy is the pride, rage, and self-pity that is welling up inside your own heart. Your battle is not to win the argument, but to crucify your own sinful nature.

Tactic 3: Anchor Your Identity. The hit only hurts if it strikes an insecurity. Remind yourself, in that very moment, of the truth: "My worth is not based on this person's opinion. My identity as a beloved son of God is non-negotiable. I am hidden with Christ in God. This insult cannot touch who I truly am." A man who knows who he is cannot be controlled by the praise or the criticism of others.

Tactic 4: Seek the Lesson, Not the Victory. Instead of asking, "How can I win?" ask a different question: "God, what do you want me to learn here?" Is there a kernel of truth in the criticism that I need to humbly accept? Is this an opportunity to practice patience? Is this a test of my character? Shifting from a defensive posture to a learning posture disarms the power of the insult.

Tactic 5: Respond, Don't React. A reaction is driven by instinct and emotion. A response is driven by wisdom and purpose. If a response is required, it should be calm, measured, and aimed at de-escalation, not victory. Often, the most powerful response is a gentle answer, as we will see in the next chapter. Other times, the most powerful response is the dignified silence of a king who refuses to get in the mud with a man throwing rocks.

The Victory of the Second Cheek

The world believes that the man who gets the last word, the man who wins the fight, is the victor. The Kingdom of God has a different definition of victory. The victory of the meek warrior is not in proving his enemy wrong, but in reflecting the character of his King.

The ultimate example is Jesus on the cross. He absorbed the ultimate hit. He took the mockery of the soldiers, the scorn of the crowd, the betrayal of his friends, and the full, crushing weight of all the sin of all humanity for all time. He had at his disposal twelve legions of angels. He could have incinerated the entire planet with a single word.

Instead, He absorbed it all. And from that place of ultimate suffering, He secured the ultimate victory, not by cursing his enemies, but by praying for them:

"Father, forgive them; for they do not know what they are doing" (Luke 23:34).

This is our standard. This is the strength to which we are called. It is the strength to suffer wrongly, to turn the other cheek, to absorb the hit, and in doing so, to show the world a power that it does not understand.

Chapter 13:
The Power of a Gentle Answer

---

*"To choose a gentle answer in the face
of wrath is not weakness. It is the
ultimate display of power under control."*

IN THE HEAT of conflict, when tensions are high and anger is flaring, the world knows only one way to communicate: escalate. The voices get louder. The words get sharper. The goal is to overwhelm, to dominate, to win the argument through sheer verbal force. It is a battle of attrition where the last man shouting is declared the victor. This is the logic of fools, and it is the soundtrack of our broken world, from the halls of power to the comments section of a YouTube video.

The spiritual warrior, however, has been trained in a different, more sophisticated form of engagement. He has been given access to a weapon so powerful that it can disarm an enraged opponent, defuse a volatile situation, and win a lasting victory without ever firing a shot in anger. It is a weapon that requires immense self-control to wield effectively. It is the tactical application of a gentle answer.

The book of Proverbs, the inspired guide for practical wisdom, lays out the principle with stunning clarity and simplicity:

"A gentle answer turns away wrath, but a harsh word stirs up anger." (Proverbs 15:1).

This is not a sentimental platitude. It is a statement of strategic, psychological, and spiritual reality. It is one of the most important principles of engagement a man will ever learn. A harsh word is like throwing gasoline on a fire. It is an instinctive, foolish, and destructive reaction that only makes the situation worse. A gentle answer is like a fire extinguisher. It is a conscious, disciplined, and powerful response that robs the fire of its oxygen and creates the space for peace.

To choose a gentle answer in the face of wrath is not weakness. It is the ultimate display of power under control. It is the mark of a man who is the master of his own spirit, a man too strong to be provoked into a petty shouting match. He is fighting for a different objective. He is not trying to win the argument; he is trying to win the relationship. And he knows that the gentle answer is his most effective tool.

The Broken Models: The Scrapper and The Silent Seether

As always, the path of meekness is a narrow road between two ditches. In the world of communication, these ditches are represented by two flawed and destructive personalities.

1. The Scrapper: The Man Who Loves to Fight

The scrapper sees every conversation as a potential debate, and every debate as a fight to the death. He is addicted to the adrenaline of argument. He listens not to understand, but to reload. He is the man who constantly plays devil's advocate, who is quick to find the flaw in any statement, who seems to derive a perverse sense of energy from conflict.

His primary weapon is the harsh word. He uses sarcasm, condescension, and interruption as his tools of the trade. He may be intelligent, but his intelligence is weaponized for the purpose of proving his own superiority. He wins a lot of arguments, but he has very few deep, trusting relationships. People learn to be guarded around him, to keep conversations superficial, because they know that any genuine opinion is likely to be met with an attack.

The scrapper thinks he is strong because he is a skilled debater. In reality, he is weak. His identity is so tied to being "right" that he sacrifices his relationships on the altar of his own ego. He is a verbal bulldozer, and like all bulldozers, he is good at demolition but terrible at building anything of lasting value.

2. The Silent Seether:
The Man Who Fights with Quiet Contempt

The silent seether is the polar opposite of the scrapper, but he is no less destructive. He avoids harsh words, but not out of strength or gentleness. He avoids them out of a passive aggressive fear of direct conflict. He doesn't escalate with angry words; he de-escalates with a cold, punishing silence.

His gentleness is a mask for contempt. When he is angered, he doesn't shout. He withdraws. He gives the silent treatment. He answers in monosyllables. His "gentleness" is a weapon designed to make the other person feel punished, isolated, and insignificant. He is not turning away wrath; he is simply storing it, letting it marinate in bitterness and resentment.

This man is not practicing meekness; he is practicing a cowardly form of manipulation. His quietness is not the calm of a controlled spirit, but the eerie quiet of a pressure cooker building toward an inevitable explosion. While the scrapper destroys relationships with explosions, the silent seether destroys them with a slow, toxic leak.

The meek warrior rejects both of these paths. He is not an aggressive debater, and he is not a passive aggressive manipulator. He is a man who has the courage to engage in difficult conversations and the strength to do so with a spirit of genuine, life-giving gentleness.

Case Study: Gideon's De-escalation

For a model in the tactical application of a gentle answer, we turn to the life of Gideon, one of the great warrior-judges of Israel. Gideon has just won a stunning, miraculous victory over the Midianite army with only 300 men. It is a moment of national triumph.

But immediately following this great victory, he is confronted with a crisis from within his own ranks. The men from the tribe of Ephraim, a powerful and proud tribe, come to him in a rage. They are furious that they were not called to the main battle, feeling that their honor has been slighted. The Bible says they

"contended with him vehemently." (Judges 8:1).

This was not a polite disagreement. This was a hostile, aggressive confrontation that was teetering on the edge of a civil war.

The men of Ephraim are coming at Gideon with harsh words, fueled by pride and jealousy. Gideon, fresh off a massive military victory, could have easily met their aggression with his own. He was the hero of the hour. He had God on his side. He could have played the scrapper, put them in their place, and asserted his authority. "Who are you to question me? Where were you when we were facing the enemy? I am the leader God has chosen. Fall in line, or I will make you fall in line." This would have been the response of a man like Saul.

Instead, Gideon deploys the gentle answer. It is a stunning piece of verbal jiu-jitsu. He doesn't defend himself. He doesn't counter attack. He humbly and strategically redirects the conversation to *their* honor. He replies:

"What have I done now in comparison with you? Is not the gleaning of the grapes of Ephraim better than the vintage of Abiezer?" (Judges 8:2).

Let's break down this masterful response. "Abiezer" was Gideon's small, insignificant clan. He is essentially saying, "My great victory is nothing compared to your small one. What you guys did in the cleanup operation (the gleaning) is more impressive than what my whole clan did in the main event (the vintage)."

He then continues, *"God has given the leaders of Midian, Oreb and Zeeb, into your hands; and what was I able to do in comparison with you?"* He gives them the credit for capturing the enemy princes. He minimizes his own role and maximizes theirs. He intentionally makes himself small to make them feel big.

The result is immediate and decisive: *"Then their anger toward him subsided when he said that."* (Judges 8:3).

With a few sentences of humble, gentle, and affirming words, Gideon completely disarmed a volatile and dangerous situation. He turned away their wrath. He did not win the argument; he won the peace. He preserved the unity of his people. This was not the act of a weak or cowardly man. This was the act of a supremely confident and wise warrior who understood that his mission - the safety of his nation - was more important than his own ego. He was strong enough to make himself small for the sake of a greater good.

The Tactical Field Manual: Deploying the Gentle Answer

This kind of response requires training. It is a spiritual discipline that must be practiced until it becomes your default setting in moments of conflict.

Tactic 1: In Your Marriage. Your marriage is the primary training ground for this principle. An argument with your spouse is a sacred opportunity to choose connection over being right.

Harsh Word (Scrapper): "You *always* do this! Why can't you just listen to me for once?" (This is an accusation. It uses absolute language and questions your spouse's character.)

Harsh Silence (Silent Seether): She expresses a frustration. You say "Fine," turn up the TV, and emotionally abandon the conversation.

Gentle Answer (Meek Warrior): "Okay, I can see that I really hurt you. That was not my intention. Can you help me understand what you felt when I said that?" (This validates her feeling, takes responsibility for the impact, and invites further, calmer conversation. It lowers your weapon and asks for a truce.)

Tactic 2: In Your Parenting. Communicating with a teenager who is pushing boundaries can feel like walking through a minefield. Your response can either escalate the conflict or build a bridge.

Harsh Word: "Don't you dare talk to me with that tone! As long as you live under my roof, you will respect me!" (This turns the conversation into a power struggle, which a teenager is often eager to fight.)

Gentle Answer: "Whoa. Your tone of voice is telling me that you are really angry right now. Let's both take a breath. I want to hear what's going on, but I need you to speak to me respectfully. Let's try this again." (This separates the issue from the tone, acknowledges their emotion, sets a clear boundary, and offers a path to a productive conversation. It maintains your authority without escalating the anger.)

Tactic 3: In the Digital Arena. Social media and email are breeding grounds for harsh words because we are disconnected from the humanity of the person on the other side of the screen.

Harsh Word: You fire back a sarcastic, condescending email, "cc-ing" the person's boss to make sure they are properly put in their place.

Gentle Answer: You receive a critical email from a colleague. Instead of replying-all with a lengthy defense, you pick up the phone and say, "Hey, I got your email. It sounds like you have some serious concerns. I'd love to hear more about them and see how we can solve this." (This takes the conflict offline, affirms their perspective, and shifts the dynamic from adversarial to collaborative. It is a power move that completely changes the rules of the game.)

When attacked online, the gentle warrior remembers his witness is at stake. Instead of getting into a mud-slinging contest, a gentle answer might be: "I appreciate you sharing your perspective. I see it differently, but I respect your right to disagree," followed by a dignified silence. You are not obligated to attend every argument you are invited to.

The Strength to De-escalate

The world is drowning in wrath. It is fueled by harsh words spoken in anger, pride, and fear. The meek warrior is called to be a combatant for peace. He is the man in the room who has the strength to absorb the anger, the wisdom to choose his words carefully, and the humility to value the relationship more than the victory.

Wielding the weapon of a gentle answer is not easy. It will require you to crucify your pride. It will demand that you trust God to be your defender. It will mean choosing to lose an argument in order to win a soul. But it is the way of your King. It is the way of the man who, when faced with the wrath of an entire world, offered not a harsh rebuttal, but a gentle invitation: "Father, forgive them." This is our model. This is our mission. This is the quiet, world-changing power of a gentle answer.

Chapter 14
The Warrior's Training Regimen

*"The discipline of fasting is a declaration
of war against this internal tyranny."*

NO SOLDIER IS sent to the front lines without first enduring the rigors of basic training. No elite athlete steps onto the field of competition without first spending countless hours in the gym, on the track, and in the film room. Victory in the moment of conflict is the direct result of discipline in the moments of preparation. You don't rise to the level of the occasion; you fall to the level of your training.

For the spiritual warrior, this principle is an iron law. The battles we have been discussing - the fight against pride, the skirmishes in our marriages, the strategic challenges at work - are not won by accident. They are won by men who have intentionally and consistently trained their souls for the rigors of spiritual combat.

Shane W. Cunningham

The world scoffs at the idea of spiritual discipline. It associates it with the passive, cloistered life of a monk, detached from the realities of the modern world. This is a profound misunderstanding. The spiritual disciplines of the Christian faith are not a retreat from the world; they are the warrior's training camp. They are the gym, the practice field, and the firing range for the soul. They are the active, rigorous, and often grueling exercises that forge the character of a man who intends to follow Jesus Christ into the brokenness of the world and fight for the Kingdom of God.

The Apostle Paul, a man who understood spiritual combat better than almost anyone, gave this direct command to his young protégé, Timothy:

"Discipline yourself for the purpose of godliness." (1 Timothy 4:7b).

The word for "discipline" here is the Greek word *gumnazō*, from which we get our word "gymnasium." The instruction is clear: Train. Work out. Put in the reps. Godliness - the state of reflecting the character of God, which includes the meekness of Christ - is not a default setting. It is the result of intentional, disciplined effort, empowered by the grace of God.

A man who wants to be physically strong does not simply wish for muscles. He goes to the gym. He lifts heavy things.

He pushes his body past its comfort zone. A man who wants to be spiritually strong must do the same for his soul. This chapter is our training manual. We will focus on three foundational disciplines that are essential for forging the quiet, unbreakable strength of a meek warrior: Solitude and Silence, Fasting, and the radical act of Praying for Your Enemies.

The Strategic Withdrawal:
The Discipline of Solitude and Silence

The modern world is a battlefield of noise. From the moment we wake up to the moment we fall asleep, we are under a constant barrage of information, opinion, and distraction. Our phones buzz with notifications. Our feeds are an endless scroll of outrage and entertainment. Our minds are saturated with podcasts, news headlines, and the curated perfection of other people's lives.

This constant state of input creates a constant state of reaction. We are anxious, agitated, and easily provoked. We have lost the ability to think deeply, to be present with our own families, and most importantly, to hear the still, small voice of our Commanding Officer. A soldier who cannot hear his commander's orders is a liability on the battlefield.

The first and most fundamental training exercise for the meek warrior is the strategic withdrawal. It is the discipline of intentionally pulling back from the noise of the world to enter into solitude and silence. This is not an escape. It is a tactical maneuver. We pull back not to run from the battle, but to recalibrate, to re-arm, and to receive our marching orders so we can re-engage with greater focus and strength.

Why It Builds Meekness: The disciplines of solitude and silence are a direct assault on the ego. Pride needs an audience. It thrives on performance, on being seen, on being heard. In the quiet, there is no one to impress. When you are alone and silent before God, you are forced to confront the man you actually are, stripped of the props of your job title, your social media profile, and your reputation.

Silence Starves Pride: In the silence, you can no longer use your words to justify, defend, or promote yourself. You are simply there, a creature before his Creator. It is in this silence that the ugly whispers of your own pride, insecurity, and fear become audible. And it is only when you can hear the enemy in your own heart that you can begin to fight him.

Solitude Breeds Dependence: When you are alone, you are reminded that you are not in control. You are not the center of the universe. This is a terrifying thought for the proud man, but it is a deeply comforting one for the warrior who knows his Commander. Solitude forces us to find our value not in our performance for others, but in our position as a beloved son of God.

Quiet is the Frequency of Command: God can and does speak through the thunder, but His most common frequency is the whisper. Elijah found God not in the wind, the earthquake, or the fire, but in a "still small voice" (1 Kings 19:12). If we do not intentionally create quiet in our lives, we will miss His guidance, His comfort, and His correction.

The Training Drills

This discipline must be practiced intentionally.

The 15-Minute Patrol: Start small. Find a time each day to sit for 15 minutes in a quiet place. No phone. No Bible. No journal. No music. Just you, the silence, and God. At first, it will feel agonizing. Your mind will race. The goal is not to have a profound spiritual experience. The goal is to simply endure the quiet. You are training your soul to be still.

The Audio Blackout: Choose one commute, one workout, or one walk each week and do it without any audio input. No podcast. No music. No audiobook. Allow your mind to process, to pray, to simply be.

The Monthly Reconnaissance: Once a month, schedule a two-to-three-hour block of time to get away by yourself. Go to a park, a library, or a quiet coffee shop. Use this time to read, pray, and think deeply about your life, your mission, and your relationship with God. This is your time to look at the strategic map of your life with your Commander.

Mastering the Appetites: The Discipline of Fasting

The spiritual warrior understands that he is engaged in a two-front war. There is the enemy without, but there is also the enemy within: the desires of his own flesh. Our bodies are not evil, but our appetites - for food, for comfort, for pleasure, for approval - are relentless and, if left unchecked, will enslave our spirit. We become mastered by our own desires.

The discipline of fasting is a declaration of war against this internal tyranny. In its simplest form, fasting is the voluntary abstention from food for a spiritual purpose. It is the warrior consciously and intentionally choosing to deny his body's most basic and powerful craving in order to feast on something greater. It is a physical act with a profound spiritual consequence.

Why It Builds Meekness: Fasting is the ultimate training exercise in saying "no" to the self. And a man who cannot say "no" to himself cannot say "yes" to God.

It Establishes Command: Every time you feel a hunger pang during a fast and choose to pray instead of eat, you are exercising a spiritual muscle. You are reminding your body,

"You are a good servant, but you are a terrible master. My spirit, submitted to God, is in command here." It is a visceral, powerful way to subordinate the physical to the spiritual.

It Exposes Your True Master: When you remove your go-to comfort (food), you are forced to see what you really rely on to manage your emotions. Do you eat when you are stressed? Bored? Sad? The discomfort of fasting shines a spotlight on the idols of your heart, the things you turn to for comfort and control instead of turning to God. This self-awareness is the first step toward true humility.

It Sharpens Your Spiritual Senses: There is a reason that, throughout Scripture and church history, fasting is consistently linked with seeking God in moments of desperation and decision. Denying the body has a way of clarifying the spirit. It strips away the dullness of a life of constant consumption and makes you more sensitive to the presence and guidance of God.

The Training Drills

If you have any medical conditions, consult your doctor before beginning.

The Single-Meal Fast: This is the entry point. Choose one day a week and skip one meal (usually lunch). Use the time you would have spent eating to read Scripture and pray.

The 24-Hour Fast: This is the next level. This can be done from sun-up to sun-up, or from dinner one day to dinner the next. Drink plenty of water. The goal is not to achieve a feat of endurance, but to use the extended period of physical denial to create an extended period of spiritual focus.

The Media Fast: Fasting is not limited to food. One of the most powerful fasts for the modern man is a fast from media. This could be a 24-hour fast from all screens, a week-long fast from social media, or a month-long fast from a particular form of entertainment like video games or Netflix. You will be astonished at how much time and mental energy is freed up for more important things.

The Unthinkable Offense:
The Discipline of Praying for Your Enemies

This is the advanced course. This is the heavy lifting of the soul. It is the discipline that separates the serious warrior from the casual recruit. In Chapter 12, we talked about the strength to absorb a hit. This discipline takes it a step further. It is the offensive maneuver of meeting hatred with a radical, supernatural act of love. Jesus gives the command in the clearest possible terms:

"But I say to you, love your enemies and pray for those who persecute you." (Matthew 5:44).

Let's be clear. This is not natural. It is not logical. It goes against every fiber of our being. Our instinct is to curse our enemies, to wish for their failure, to savor the thought of their eventual downfall. To actively and genuinely pray for the blessing, the good, and the redemption of someone who has hurt you is perhaps the most difficult command in all of Scripture. And that is precisely why it is such a powerful tool for forging meekness.

Why It Builds Meekness: Praying for your enemies is a direct, violent assault on the fortress of your own pride.

It Forces You to Surrender Justice: When you pray for your enemy, you are formally handing their case over to God. You are relinquishing your self-appointed role as judge, jury, and executioner. You are admitting that God's justice is perfect and your desire for revenge is not. This is an act of profound surrender.

It Breaks the Power of Bitterness: You cannot hold onto a root of bitterness toward someone while simultaneously and sincerely praying for God's blessing upon them. The act of prayer is spiritual chemotherapy. It attacks the cancerous cells of resentment and unforgiveness in your soul. The prayer may feel fake and forced at first, but if you persist, God will use the discipline to perform surgery on your heart.

It Aligns Your Heart with God's: God's desire is not for the destruction of the wicked, but that they would turn from their ways and live (Ezekiel 33:11). When you pray for your enemy's salvation and well-being, you are aligning your will with God's will. You are beginning to see them not as a monster, but as a broken person, made in the image of God, for whom Christ also died. This is the pinnacle of humility.

The Training Drills

Identify Your Target: Be specific. Who is the person whose name makes your stomach clench? The colleague who betrayed you? The family member who wounded you? The public figure you despise? Write their name down.

Formulate the Prayer: Do not pray, "Lord, show them how wrong they were." That is still a prayer of pride. Pray for their blessing. "Lord, I pray for John. Bless his family. Give him health. Prosper his work. And most of all, Lord, draw his heart to you. Show him your love and your mercy."

Engage with Consistency: Commit to praying this prayer every day for thirty days. Keep a journal of how your feelings toward that person begin to change. This will be some of the hardest spiritual work you ever do. And it will be some of the most liberating.

These disciplines are not a checklist for earning God's favor. You are already fully loved and accepted in Christ. Think of them as the necessary training that allows you to live out the reality of who you already are. You are a warrior. Now it's time to train like one. The battle for meekness is not won when the insult is hurled; it is won in the quiet of the morning, on your knees, when no one is watching.

Shane W. Cunningham

Chapter 15
The Teachable Heart

"His inability to receive correction, to humbly admit his fault, and to repent was his ultimate disqualification as a leader."

WE HAVE COME to the end of our journey together. We have dismantled the lie that meekness is weakness and replaced it with the biblical truth that it is power under perfect control. We have walked with kings and prophets, apostles and generals. We have crafted a battle plan for our homes, our workplaces, and our own souls. We have established a training regimen to build the spiritual muscle required for the mission.

But there is one final quality we must discuss. It is the attribute that ties everything else together. It is the essential posture that a warrior must maintain for his entire life if he is to finish his race well. It is the spiritual immune system that protects him from the terminal disease of pride. It is the single greatest indicator of a man's potential for lifelong growth.

It is the quality of a teachable heart.

A man can have a brilliant mind, a charismatic personality, and a warehouse of spiritual gifts, but if his heart is unteachable, he is a liability. He is a man who has stopped growing, and a warrior who is not advancing is, by definition, retreating. The meek warrior, the man who wants to be useful to his King for the duration of the war, must fiercely cultivate a heart that is humble, open, and eager to be corrected. This is not the final chapter of a program to be completed; it is the foundational mindset for a race that is never over until we cross the finish line.

The Tragedy of the Closed Mind:
A Final Look at Saul

To understand the life-and-death importance of a teachable heart, we must return one last time to the tragic figure of King Saul. His story is not just a warning against disobedience; it is a profound and heartbreaking portrait of an unteachable spirit. His downfall was not a single, catastrophic event, but a slow, hardening process. It was a series of moments where he was offered the gift of correction and refused to receive it.

The first major crack in his leadership appeared early in his reign. The Philistine army was gathered for war, and Saul and his small, terrified army were waiting for the prophet Samuel to come and offer the pre-battle sacrifice. But Samuel was late. The troops were deserting. The pressure was mounting. Saul, in a moment of fear and impatience, took matters into his own hands and offered the sacrifice himself - a direct violation of God's command.

When Samuel finally arrived, the confrontation was telling. Did Saul confess his sin? No. He made excuses.

"I saw that the people were scattering from me... so I forced myself and offered the burnt offering." (1 Samuel 13:11-12).

He blamed his circumstances. He blamed the people. He portrayed himself as a victim of the situation. He could not, or would not, simply say, "I was afraid, and I sinned." His heart was already beginning to harden.

But the definitive, final test came in his campaign against the Amalekites. The command from God, delivered through Samuel, was severe and absolute: utterly destroy everything and everyone. Spare nothing. It was a holy judgment.

Saul obeyed, but only partially. He and his army destroyed what was worthless, but they kept the best of the sheep, the oxen, and the king, Agag, alive. It was a compromise born of greed and a desire to please the people.

When Samuel confronted him, we are given a prime example of an unteachable heart. Saul's response is a textbook case of evasion and self-deception.

First, he lies. His opening statement to the prophet is a blatant falsehood:

"I have carried out the command of the LORD." (1 Samuel 15:13).

Then, he deflects. When Samuel points out the sound of bleating sheep, Saul immediately shifts the blame:

"The people took some of the spoil... to sacrifice to the LORD your God." (1 Samuel 15:15, 21).

It wasn't me, it was them. And they did it for a good, religious reason! He wraps his disobedience in a cloak of piety. Finally, he minimizes. He sees his sin not as rebellion against the King of the Universe, but as a minor administrative error.

It is in this moment that Samuel delivers one of the most famous and devastating rebukes in all of Scripture:

"Does the LORD delight in burnt offerings and sacrifices as much as in obeying the voice of the LORD? Behold, to obey

is better than sacrifice, and to heed than the fat of rams. For rebellion is as the sin of witchcraft, and insubordination is as iniquity and idolatry. Because you have rejected the word of the LORD, He has also rejected you from being king." (1 Samuel 15:22-23).

Saul's unteachable heart was the root of his rebellion. His inability to receive correction, to humbly admit his fault, and to repent was his ultimate disqualification as a leader.

Now, contrast this with David. Years later, after his horrific sin with Bathsheba and the murder of her husband, the prophet Nathan confronted him with a blistering parable. David, unlike Saul, did not make excuses. He did not blame Bathsheba. He did not justify his actions. His response was immediate, total, and heartbreakingly simple:

"I have sinned against the LORD." (2 Samuel 12:13).

This is the sound of a teachable heart. It is the sound of a man who, when shown his sin, breaks instead of bristles. This is why God could redeem and restore David, and why Saul was left to spiral into madness and despair.

The Anatomy of a Teachable Heart

A teachable heart is not a personality type. It is a spiritual posture, a set of conscious choices that a man makes every single day. It has three key components.

1. The Humility to Listen

It all begins here - a teachable man operates from the humble assumption that he does not have all the answers. He understands the wisdom of Proverbs:

"The way of a fool is right in his own eyes, but a wise man is he who listens to counsel." (Proverbs 12:15).

This kind of listening is an active, not a passive, skill. It is the discipline of silencing your own inner monologue, your desire to be right, and your need to formulate a rebuttal, in order to truly enter another person's perspective. A teachable man seeks out wise counsel. He has older men in his life that he looks up to. He listens to his wife, recognizing that she has a perspective on his life and character that no one else possesses. He doesn't surround himself with "yes-men" who will only tell him what he wants to hear. He surrounds himself with people who love him enough to tell him the truth.

2. The Courage to Be Wrong

For many men, the three hardest words in the English language are, "I was wrong." We have been conditioned to believe that admitting fault is a sign of weakness, a failure of leadership. The meek warrior knows that the exact opposite is true.

It takes immense strength and profound courage to own your mistakes. It is the insecure man, the man whose identity is built on a fragile foundation of performance and approval, who must defend his every decision at all costs. His ego cannot afford the hit. But the man whose identity is securely anchored in his status as a beloved, forgiven son of God is free. He can afford to be wrong. His worth is not on the line.

A leader - whether a father, a husband, or a boss - who can genuinely say "I was wrong, and I am sorry" creates a culture of grace and safety around him. It gives everyone else permission to be human. It demolishes the destructive pretense of perfection and builds a foundation of trust. It is one of the most powerful leadership tools in the world.

3. The Eagerness for Correction

This is the highest level of a teachable heart. It is one thing to humbly accept correction when it is brought to you. It is another thing entirely to proactively seek it out. A truly teachable man does not fear criticism; he sees it as a priceless gift. He understands that his blind spots are, by definition, invisible to him. He needs the eyes of trusted brothers and sisters to help him see himself clearly.

This man is not afraid to ask the hard questions:

To his wife: "How am I really doing as a husband? Where am I falling short? What is one thing I could do to love you better?"

To his children: "Have I been fair with you? Have I provoked you to anger? Do you feel like you can talk to me?"

To a trusted friend or mentor: "What is the biggest area of weakness you see in my life right now? Where do I need to grow?"

To ask these questions, and to listen to the answers without becoming defensive, requires a level of meekness that is forged only in the fires of deep communion with God. It is the posture of a man who is more committed to his own sanctification than he is to his own comfort.

The Training Ground for a Teachable Heart

This kind of heart does not develop by accident. It must be intentionally cultivated.

1. The Word as a Mirror

The primary tool for cultivating a teachable heart is a daily, humble engagement with the Word of God. The book of James says that the man who hears the word but does not do what it says is like a man who looks at his face in a mirror and then immediately forgets what he looks like. But the man who

"Looks intently into the perfect law, the law of liberty, and continues in it... this man will be blessed in what he does." (James 1:25).

The Bible is our mirror. We must come to it each day not just to learn information, but to be changed. Our prayer as we read should be the prayer of the psalmist:

"Search me, O God, and know my heart; try me and know my anxious thoughts; and see if there be any hurtful way in me, and lead me in the everlasting way." (Psalm 139:23-24).

2. The Practice of Confession

Make the act of saying "I was wrong" a regular spiritual discipline. The more you do it, the less power your pride has over you. Start by confessing to God daily, being specific about your sins. Then, when you have wronged someone, make it your immediate practice to go to them and make it right. Do not let the sun go down on your anger or your pride. This practice will keep your heart soft and pliable before God and man.

3. The Pursuit of Wisdom

Actively seek out the company of people who are wiser and more godly than you are. The book of Proverbs reminds us,

"He who walks with wise men will be wise, but the companion of fools will suffer harm." (Proverbs 13:20).

Resist the urge to only spend time with people who think exactly like you. Find men who will challenge you, sharpen you, and push you to be more like Christ.

The Lifelong Advance

The journey of the spiritual warrior is not a short sprint; it is a long, grueling marathon. The moment a man believes he has "arrived" - that he has mastered meekness, that he has no more room to grow - is the moment he has stepped onto the same path that led King Saul to ruin.

The teachable heart is the engine of the lifelong advance. It is the humble, hungry, and relentless desire to be conformed more and more into the image of Jesus Christ. A man with a teachable heart will stumble, he will fail, and he will be corrected. But he will never be defeated, because every stumble becomes an opportunity to learn, every failure a chance to receive grace, and every correction a gift that makes him stronger, wiser, and more useful to his King.

This is the final mark of the meek warrior. He is a man who knows that he is a masterpiece in the making, and he humbly submits to the hands of the Master Craftsman, knowing that the work will not be complete until the day he sees Him face to face.

Epilogue
The Quiet Roar

WE STARTED THIS book with a problem. The word "meek" has been stolen, stripped of its power, and handed back to us as a synonym for "weak." We've been handed a picture of a man who is harmless, passive, and soft - a man who is completely irrelevant in a world that respects only strength.

Our mission has been to take that word back.

Together, we've taken it to the forge of Scripture and hammered it back into its true shape. We've seen that meekness is not the absence of power, but the restraining of it. It's the quiet, controlled strength of a lion who walks beside his master, a creature of immense capability who has willingly placed his power under a greater command.

We found this truth in the lives of history's greatest warriors. We saw it in David, the giant-slayer who refused to kill his vulnerable enemy. We saw it in Moses, the general whose power was forged in the humility of the desert. We saw it in the Apostle Paul, a human dynamo who harnessed his ferocious zeal for the sake of the gospel. And we saw its perfect expression in Jesus Christ, the Lion of Judah, whose greatest display of strength was the voluntary submission of the cross.

We then carried this re-forged weapon into the battles of our own lives. We learned that this gentle strength is the key to leading our families, to excelling in our work, and to navigating a world of conflict and criticism. We established a training regimen for the soul, because this kind of strength is not born of instinct, but of discipline.

And now, this book ends, but your mission begins.

This was never meant to be a collection of interesting ideas. It is a summons. It is a call to step out of the shallow stream of contemporary manhood and into the deep river of true, biblical strength. It is a call to become the kind of man the world desperately needs but no longer knows how to build.

You will not be perfect. You will feel the old instincts rise up - the pride that bristles at criticism, the anger that lashes out with a harsh word, the fear that chooses passivity over courage. In those moments of failure, do not retreat in shame. Run to the King. His grace is not a safety net for the perfect; it is the field hospital for the wounded warrior. It is there you will find the forgiveness and strength to get back in the fight.

The world already has enough men who roar to defend their own egos. It is starving for men whose strength creates safety for others. It needs men whose confidence is so deeply rooted in Christ that they have nothing to prove. It needs men whose quiet roar of integrity, service, and self-control is louder and more world-changing than all the angry shouting of the proud.

You have been given the standard. You know the mission.

It is time to go live it.

About the Author

Shane W. Cunningham writes for two distinct battlefields: the complex spiritual life of the Christian warrior and the developing heart of a child.

A former United States Marine, Shane served in intelligence and counterintelligence at high levels of national security, including the Pentagon and various agencies. This background gives him a unique, strategic perspective that he now applies to the spiritual realm. For adults, he authors non-fiction guides such as The Military Guide to Spiritual Warfare and Meek Isn't Weak. These books are designed to equip believers with a resilient, warrior mentality, ready to engage in the spiritual battles of modern life.

As a husband and a father to his children, Jaxon and Lorelei, Shane's mission extends to the next generation. He is passionate about creating fun, thought-provoking books that instill a strong foundation of faith and character in young readers such as intense thrillers like Serpent's Tooth, part of the Luke Carter Series.

He and his wife, Jessica, lead 7 Benih Ministry, a Texas-based nonprofit dedicated to supporting orphanages in Indonesia and shepherding local churches.